21

BUILDING TOMORROW
AS YOUNG ADULTS

21

BUILDING TOMORROW
AS YOUNG ADULTS

Written by
IVAN SNODGRASS

Edited by
NICK ERDOGAN

iUniverse, Inc.
Bloomington

21—BUILDING TOMORROW AS YOUNG ADULTS

iUniverse books may be ordered through booksellers or by contacting:

iUniverse
1663 Liberty Drive
Bloomington, IN 47403
www.iuniverse.com
1-800-Authors (1-800-288-4677)

ISBN: 978-1-4759-1443-6 (sc)
ISBN: 978-1-4759-1444-3 (ebk)

Printed in the United States of America

iUniverse rev. date: 04/19/2012

"A special thank you to all of those who helped me collaborate ideas and proofread as I wrote this book. I could not have done this alone."

21

Building Tomorrow As Young Adults
Table of Contents

An Informal Introduction

When picking up a book like this you may wonder *why should I read what this Ivan Snodgrass guy has to say? What puts the author of this book in any sort of position to speak on growing and learning for young adults?* There is one simple, but possibly refutable, answer to that question: I am one.

I turned 21 while writing this book and I am just another young adult trying to keep up with the ever-changing world we currently attempt to call home. Due to my environment and the values my mother placed within me, I have always questioned everything around me in my endless pursuit to understand everything I encounter and experience. This has led to many hours of self-reflection, late night contemplation, and creations like this book you are currently beginning to read.

Inside these pages you will read about 21 values, or Pillars, that I find to be important in helping us grow and prosper as young adults. These are all Pillars I feel would be incredibly beneficial to keep in mind, learn, and master with time. These are concepts that I have come to notice and appreciate from my own experiences, and they are lessons I am still learning every day. I find that no one really takes the time to write about these things as they are happening, so I thought I would give it a shot.

Why 21 Pillars? I turned 21 while writing this book and 21 is also the pivotal age for change and transformation in a young adult's life. Our years we live from eighteen to twenty four have been identified as the time period in our lives where we will do ninety percent of our changing; the time period above all others that shapes who we become. It's an important time to say the very least.

I have always enjoyed helping others. I need to do it more often. We, as young adults, will shape the future of this country and of this world. We will change the world as the world changes us; a simultaneous sculpting of one another. We can always use a word of advice or have a story shared with us, and I hope this book empowers, uplifts, or at least encourages someone. I can only hope that this book is at least worth someone's time to read from cover to cover.

I selected a format for this book based upon our generation. We learn and relate to things well if it is told as a story or if it takes on a personal format when it is presented to us. This is why I have put in a personal example or story from my own life to go along with and relate to each of the Pillars of the book. I feel like it will help many readers relate with certain topics if I open up myself and share with the reader about my own personal experiences and perspectives. It is what we do with our own friends in the car or in our own homes; we share our lives with each other. I want the reader to be able to share the experience with me, and ultimately themselves.

As the author of this book, I am not saying I have mastered these 21 pillars. It would be a stretch for me to say I have even mastered one of them. I am constantly working to be a better person for myself and those around me. I will try to keep these things in mind as life goes on, become better about sticking to what these themes stand for, and live them throughout. I am not professing to be a master, or even a teacher of this material; I simply would like to instill these 21 Pillars into your mind, and let you decide what to do from here. We can strive together.

I have always been a big fan of quotes and their short but powerful messages. They can relay so much and leave us with open-ended conversation in only a sentence or two. This is why I have peppered each chapter with applicable quotes that I feel ring out the theme of that certain Pillar. I hope it will allow for an easy takeaway and something that will become easy to recall. If we can remember a quote about a theme or message, it can usually be used in conversation and thought. That is my overall hope; that these messages could be used after you read this book.

In addition, this book could be for more than just young adults. However, lessons learned earlier in life will give us more time for them to take hold and affect us. If someone who would not consider themselves a young adult were to read this book, they could hopefully still take something great away from it. I wrote this book and aimed it at other young adults like me trying to grow up and meet the expectations of not only the world around us, but ourselves. I did this because I know what it is like in this fast-paced and crazy world we call home. We could all use a little help from someone; someone like us.

I also would like to stress that this book is not just about my past and I hope it does not come off as merely an autobiography. My stories are placed there to give you something to relate to or compare your own stories with; relating is understanding. You will learn a lot about me and who I am in this book, so there is no need to introduce myself. I hope this book can at least allow you to question or improve your own life in a positive way, no matter your age. If it at least sits well with you for a couple of days, then it is an accomplishment for me. I just want everyone to know that they can receive help, give it, and live life together. We are always learning and growing. It is what we do and who we are. I hope you enjoy this book and these Pillars, and I hope you are able to take them to heart.

IT IS ALL ABOUT
WHAT YOU KEEP
IN MIND

Our mind is a wildly complex thing,
and it is what drives us in everything that we do.
What we keep inside it, and how we utilize that,
ends up being our steering wheel we use
to journey through life.

OPINIONS ARE NOT FACTS

It seems so obvious, right? We all know that our opinions are not accepted facts of the world. It seems like common sense. However, this concept can be all too hard to keep in mind during certain situations as we exchange values and ideas with other people, especially those who disagree with us. Our opinions are our own ideas, no one else's, and nothing more.

At this point you may be thinking something: *isn't this entire book just his opinion?* Yes, these 21 Pillars, the themes, and the point of this entire book are all expressions of my opinion. There may be certain Pillars you disagree with, that you may even dislike, as you continue reading on. That would be your opinion and I would need to respect it. We all think and process things differently, and no two people will ever see the world the exact same way. Opinions consume who we are. How we translate them is what matters. It is not our opinions I want to discuss in this chapter, but rather how we choose to handle them.

Those people who flaunted their "superior" opinions around us in our lives, probably shared some of the same ideas with those around them, but it was all in their attitude and presentation. Most often, the reason we get offended by situations like these is because of the way the opinions of others are presented to us; the context, and not the substance.

> "Opinion has caused more trouble on this little earth
> than plagues or earthquakes."
> —Voltaire

There have been times when I have taken my opinions too far, and there have also been times when I felt chastised for mine. We will all experience both sides, but we just have to keep respect in mind as we encounter those in life who do not quite agree with us. It is easy to converse with another person and paint a big smile on our faces when we are in agreement. That is natural. However, when we walk on the viewpoints of those we disagree with, we lose our respect, care, and understanding. When we do that, we become those we find bothersome and our foot becomes lodged far in our mouth.

I would say that religion is one of the biggest topics of opinionated controversy in our generation; but there are also many other touchy topics out there such as politics, sexuality, and social equality, among others. But through my personal experiences, I have found religion to be the most sensitive subject of debate. A lot of the time, conversations about conflicting religious views end in flared tempers and pure frustration. Why is that?

Perhaps a lack of respect is the cause. Maybe it is the way we speak about our own opinions and the ideologies to which we cling. Is it that skin-burning defensive feeling we get because we feel like we are put on trial when confronted? Several factors go into the culmination of feelings and emotions that get evoked from this topic of debate. After all, it is quite a personal and important issue to each of us. Everyone has an idea and opinion on their religious beliefs, and we all have our own reasons. It just depends on how you choose to express yours.

My specific religious point of view, in my opinion, is irrelevant in light of this Pillar. It is how I handled opposition, disagreements, and all the things I experienced along the way that molds this Pillar into a personal story of mine. I grew up with a group of friends that was pretty evenly split on the topic of religion. I was frequently questioned why I believed the way I did, why I got to the point that I did on the issue, or how I could ever believe what I do. Some of the questionings were friendly and enlightening, and both parties were able to take something away from it. Some conversations were accusatory and became attacks on my intellectual sanity; there is a stark difference—trust me.

"Everything we hear is an opinion, not a fact. Everything we see is a perspective, not the truth."

—Marcus Aurelius

My belief on shaping the views we hold is elaborated on in *Challenge Your Own Perceptions*, but what I would like to focus on here is how people can differ in their expressions. Think about two people in your life. Picture that one person you know who could disagree with you, talk things through with you, but then you both learn from each other and still walk away pleased with the conversation. It is a nice feeling to be respected like that, is it not? Now, the other person: that individual who frustrates you to no end any time the two of you disagree on a topic. Notice the difference? You will the next time it happens.

The classic duo of politics and religion is a powerful set of topics for this Pillar. In fact, it can be so affecting to many people, that I have heard countless individuals refuse to discuss their political or religious beliefs with others. I have also seen people sever relationships with others because of disagreements on these topics. Why would people not be willing to talk about things that mean so much to them inside? It is probably because of how they felt when they opened up their mouth in the face of opposition. They were probably slammed for their core values and ideologies by someone else, and it bruised them on these topics altogether. To me, it is saddening when I hear someone say they will not express their views anymore, because I just have to think: I wonder exactly what it is that they have been through already with defending their opinion?

I have been brought to tears by those who talked to me like I was a no-good dog for my political and religious views. People may not have meant to be so hurtful, but it is easy for tempers to flare during talks like these. I have seen friends and acquaintances of mine withdraw themselves and become embarrassed because of the pretentious presentation of opinions by other people. So, if we all kept in mind that our opinions are the furthest thing from facts, maybe we could all share ourselves with other people surrounding us more than we already do, and get along while doing so.

"The greatest deception men suffer is from their own opinions."

—Leonardo da Vinci

Next time you start speaking out about a religious or political stance you take, do it with everyone else in mind. These can be touchy and very personal subjects for many people, and an understanding mindset will always help calm the seas. There is a reason you think the way you do, and that same rule applies to more than six billion other people. We each believe the way we do because that is simply who we are. No two people are exactly the same, right? No two sets of opinions will be identical either, and we just need to learn how to deal with that.

There are countless examples of opinions laced with factual stitching. Are any of them coming to mind? Think about your own values. How do you present them to others? Is the first sentence out of your mouth a loud and boastful one, saying how things are and you know exactly why? Or do you go about life in a more courteous and understanding manner? I am sure the people around you know exactly how you present yourself. They are, after all, the ones who have to put up with your opinions.

"People seem not to see that their opinion of the world is also a confession of character."

—Ralph Waldo Emerson

A pet peeve of mine, something I feel is just one of hundreds of examples of misrepresented opinions, is the under-use of the simple phrase "I think." Examples include: *that band is stupid. That movie sucked. She is a tool, and a disgrace. He is an idiot.* Sound familiar? It is how we sometimes talk, is it not? But think about this: *I thought that movie sucked.* Still a little upfront, but a little better, right? There is a little more respect, and grace to a statement like that. Saying *I think* makes a simple yet profound difference when we are talking about our views with others. *I think* it shows that we know what we are saying is merely an opinion, not one dressed up as a fact. There are hundreds of ways we could try to be more understanding within our ideals. That is, again, just one of my very own opinions.

Finding out, when you are twenty years old, that you will never know your biological father can change your perspective quite a bit, (this is elaborated in *Hold Respect for Others*). I remember growing up and hearing others being told, "You're adopted" in school, as if it were some sort of zestful joke. That saying now carries a whole new significance with me since I found out about my own situation with my father. In addition to minor things like that, my viewpoint on sperm donations and similar processes has obviously gone through some reformation as well.

I got into a conversation one evening with several friends of mine discussing current events topics like abortion and adoption. I specifically remember hearing one of my friends saying "I would never donate to a sperm bank, because that stuff is just plain creepy." He did not know about my genetic situation, that I was a sperm donor baby. My friend did not know that I have never met my biological father, but in fact, if it was not for my biological father's donation, I would not be here today. He did not really pick up on the offense I had taken when he had said that. He said things like sperm donations were weird and he could never adopt or raise someone else's child after an artificial insemination. He is entitled to his opinion, but it was the way that he presented it that made me feel weird and out-casted. We will not always know the opinions or life stories of others, so watching the way we talk about our opinions could be, at minimum, considered an act of courtesy.

There are hundreds of scenarios that I could point out and spotlight a way in which we can be courteous and understanding with our opinions. Some may find it measly or unnecessary in the face of expression. I just find that the more often we remind ourselves that every single opinion of ours is nowhere near a fact, the easier it is to live with that in mind. So please, for yourself and all those around you, remember that our opinions are not facts, no matter how badly we may want them to be. And that, my friends, is a fact.

Everything Changes

The only constant in life is change. Sometimes we ignore or take that piece of advice for granted because of how frequently we hear it while growing up. The fact of the matter is that is it so very true. The only thing that we can do is try to keep up and enjoy the things around us as they are happening. As everything rushes by, hold on to the good, and let the bad be carried away by the passing wind.

The whole thought of everything changing is a lot like the theme of *Appreciate Now, Not Later*, except it emphasizes the externality of the whole idea. We must stress to others, as well as ourselves, that much of what changes in our lives is completely free of our control. In fact, I would say 99% of our lives are out of our own personal control. This includes everything from weather patterns and current political events to the people around us and their own personal lives. If we hardly have any control over the fact that everything changes, why is it a chapter in this book? Simply put, we need to keep in mind that nothing in our life will remain the same. It is inevitable and the best anyone can do is recognize what is happening and realize that we must just learn to go with it.

The most change occurs to people during their years as young adults. It is widely accepted that a person will go through the majority of their personal shaping and changing between the ages of eighteen and twenty-four. It is a crucial time in our lives and a time that needs to be recognized and respected. People in college often see these changes in others at a rapid pace. The time after high school is when the world attempts to sculpt and put its impressions on us. High school reunions prove this without question.

We quickly become the product of our life experiences and the externalities that surround us in our daily lives. Those things are also always changing. With me turning 21 this year, I am in the prime of this suggested time period and I sometimes notice the changes in my life as they happen. It can be very surreal.

"The only thing that is constant is change."

—Heraclitus

One of the most notable and recent ways I have noticed the changes in my life was through documents called *Weekly Reports*. I did them during my first semester as a Resident Assistant at Oklahoma State in the Zink-Allen community, starting in January of 2011. We were required to fill out a weekly report every Monday. In each report every week was six thought-provoking questions that would allow an opportunity to reflect on the past week. These questions involved things that encouraged us to consider ourselves personally and professionally in our duties as an RA. One of the questions was, "What is new with you this week?"

Looking back at all my answers now is truly astounding. I had no idea how much changed in my life every seven days. From personal relationships to events in my classes (there was always plenty to respond with on that particular question). It was usually a decent-sized paragraph. So if it makes you wonder how many changes there are in your life per week, write it down once a week and take a look. Try writing a list at the beginning of each month. You will probably be surprised.

Two years may seem like an eternity to younger children. To some of those who have lived sixty years it may seem like they blinked an eye and years had passed. Being a young adult each day seems to go by slowly, but when you stop to look back, the months and years have flown by. Why is that? I am sure there are hundreds of possible opinions and explanations for that anomaly.

For me, two years has meant everything. In the year of 2009 I was a completely different person. I had completely different values, logic, and perceptions; not to mention I hated mayonnaise and salads back then. I dated a girl for the summer that year that I would never think about giving a chance now. She was not someone who had any personal values or passion, and she tended to feed off the worries and shortcomings of others. I treated the girlfriend situation differently, took a lot of things for granted, and was very ignorant on a lot of issues and experiences in life.

If I were to try and identify one single reason I am such a completely different person now, it would be very hard. It would take me a long time to come up with an answer, and even then the answer I came up with would not even come close to justifying everything that has occurred. Not only that, but I did not just wake up one day and realize that I had changed during the course of the previous night's sleep. It happened one day at a time, experience by experience, and if I never looked back I would never have even thought about what had happened. It can be very eye-opening and intimidating. Usually all the little things that come together in the end is what ends up leading to change, not one specific reason or event. This is the key. Keep that in mind, and watch it as it happens.

If I were to hang out with the Summer 2009 version of myself, I would probably get annoyed. I would think that this kid has a lot to learn and that he needs to hold more respect. Looking back now, I used to be such a punk and I was pretty hateful to a lot of people. I was just ignorant and I frequently had times where I had no disregard for others. I thought recycling was dumb and I called people who did "hippies." Now I insist on recycling. I thought the police were annoying and nothing but a plague to an exciting time. Then I realized they will probably save my life or help me out in a great way some day. I also saw that the reasons I was hateful towards the police were for my own childish and selfish agendas, such as driving too fast down a crowded street.

I used hate speech against individuals in a joking manner and I did not think it should be curbed. I shudder at the thought now. I had racist, homophobic, sexist, and ageist tendencies that I am not proud of when I look back at my former self. The furthering of my education through two different universities, surrounding myself with people I looked up to and respected, and meeting people from all walks of life were just a few parts of my changing life that taught me something important; I desired a change within myself.

Some would say that this is happening to all of us, and that it is just part of growing up. But growing up is not something to be shrugged off. It is something to be noticed and we should all learn from it. Maybe that's our problem: too often we don't learn from our own mistakes. We should take some more time to look back and reflect on our own lives. Perhaps we could benefit from it? I think so. I know that I will try to better myself by thinking and noticing things along the way. It will allow for me to try and make sure I do not repeat the same egregious mistakes I have in years before.

> "The doors we open and close each day decide the lives we live."
> —Flora Whittemore

Let us try to keep in mind that not just the major changes in life are noteworthy. Like a puzzle, every little detail in our lives builds together to shape our life and our experiences as a whole. A building is made up of thousands, sometimes even millions, of bricks or pieces of framework. When even one piece is missing it is quite noticeable. A change is needed to patch that spot. It is the same way with the environment that surrounds us. A single conversation or phone call can shift and sculpt a relationship between two individuals, for better or for worse. A random event on the way to work or school could change you forever, and you may not even realize it. Think about this: what is changing in your life right now, no matter how big or small? Probably everything.

Everything in your life will change eventually. Some of it will occur by the end of the day. Some of it will happen by the end of the week. It is likely that all of it will have changed at least a little by the end of the year. Routines, opinions, traditions, perspectives, friends, family ties, physical characteristics, locations, desires, troubles, regrets, and much more are just several examples of what will change around us. Does this not, in effect, change us?

We would not want to wonder why we stand for something or who we are. For us to be able to be true to ourselves, I think knowing how we became who we are now is one of the most crucial parts. If we watch what changes in our day to day lives and how these alterations affect us, we can sculpt these events to shape who we may want to become down the road. We may even be able to change ourselves today if we desired to do so. Either way, it is not a question of whether we will change or not, but when and how. So hold on and enjoy the show that is Life. It only performs once.

Appreciate Now, Not Later

Do you ever find yourself stopping to enjoy the little things, smelling the roses, so to speak? When people mention these sayings they are trying to appreciate everything in life, even the littlest things, as they are happening. We cannot show our gratuity to something or someone as effectively after they are gone. Sadly, many of us never realize this until it is too late; over and over again.

As mentioned in *Learn From Your Mistakes,* for us to change the way things will affect us in our lives down the road, we will have to learn from the decisions we have made in the past. If we have already seen the effects of wishing we had said something more, treated someone differently, or appreciated something more, then we should take away something from that cognitive realization. Perhaps we should try and learn to start appreciating in the moment, not after life has already passed us by.

Little practices of this principle could make someone's day better or lend someone else a smile. Saying thank you to people when they hold a door open for you, telling the people around you at work how good of a job they do, or letting those who are close to you know how much you appreciate them can have a big impact. Let people know if they look good that day or if you appreciate something they did for you. Gratuity and appreciation go hand-in-hand quite well. Timing layers the thick and rich icing on the cake.

There are certain situations in my life that perfectly ring out the theme of this chapter when they come to mind. There are several people in my memories that I miss, and whom I wish I had been more appreciative of when they were around. Nostalgia consumes me as I think about childhood memories while growing up with old friends, surreal snapshots of every day interactions with them, and reflections on how things used to be back in the days of old. Those memories tend to flood me with appreciation each time I stir them around. There are a few situations that I wish I could change and there are fossilized relationships that will always continue to remind me of their skeletons.

"If you don't appreciate it, you don't deserve it."
—Terry Josephson

One of those relationships includes an ex-girlfriend of mine, whom I was with for two years and four months. After our relationship came to an end, she was still a close friend of mine for two years; my best friend for quite some time. None of that seems real anymore now that we are nothing but an old story. We have now become total strangers, and everything between us has become nothing but a book of memories and old photographs. She has denied the use of her name in this book so we will refer to her as Rachel.

The entire story from start to finish would be a book in itself. Instead of telling my own version of *The Odyssey*, I will only focus on one of the aspects of our entire relation. That slice of memory happens to be negative, and it reflects on everything I feel went wrong inside the mutual appreciation that was supposed to thrive between us after our romantic relationship had ended.

One of my favorite film directors, Quentin Tarantino, is famous for starting films in the middle or the end of the chronological plot progression. He shows us a crucial scene in the middle or near the end of the plot and then goes back in time to catch us up on what is happening and why. It allows for our interest to immediately become spiked, and we have all sorts of questions right off the bat. It is a really interesting effect and one he seemed to pioneer. With that being said, let me do the same with this story.

While Rachel and I were still friends, she took a certain interest in one of my friends and it didn't take long for them to start dating.

Fast-forward, and somehow we have gotten ourselves to today: Rachel's current boyfriend, my old friend, told me that if I ever spoke to either of them again, especially her, then I would have serious problems.

Got questions? Let me drag the scene back in time to 2008. This is when I ended the relationship between Rachel and I in the fall of that year. To say the least, I could have been a lot more understanding and compassionate about the break-up. We had dated for over two years, and to put it very frankly, I had lost interest in the future between us. I had "fallen out of love," so to speak, for many reasons. I did not feel like there was a lasting future between us anymore, and I wanted to remedy these sinking feelings. She begged for a chance to prove herself and change my mind, but I did not find that scenario to be a sincere proposition. I had been watching our natural relationship for the previous six months or so, and my confidence in our future had already been shot dead in its tracks. We went on a break from the relationship, but after a few weeks my decision remained the same. So our relationship ended.

Following the breakup, we remained best friends throughout the peaks and the valleys of our respectively different lives. By this point we knew everything there was to know about one-another. We each had our share of relationships during this time but remained close friends. Directly following our break-up, there was an underlying situation that started gaining traction. This situation happened to be of a negative nature and it started seeping into our daily friendship.

Some of my friends thought the only reason she stayed such a close friend of mine after our relationship was because she wanted to try and get me back. My mind did not sit well with such an idea. It seemed so torturous to be striving to get someone back while also trying to be good friends with them, and to see them come in and out of other relationships. I swayed back and forth on how I truly felt about what they were saying, Rachel's intentions, and my gut instincts. I could never truly decide and over time my indecisiveness took its toll.

This time period stretched on for over a year, and looking back, this was a time when I did not appreciate her nearly as much as I should have. If you want to talk about a loyal friend who truly cares for you, Rachel was a perfect example. If I needed to rant, someone to do homework with, a buddy to run errands with, or someone to lend me a smile and helping hand, she was always willing. Unfortunately, it often seemed like the only two people who agreed with our friendship existing in the first place, was us.

We got flak for being such close friends after having dated for over two years. Due to much of the hearsay and opinions crawling around I began to undervalue her loyalty and how much she truly cared for me as a friend of hers. These paranoid possibilities affected our friendship more than I would like to remember.

Because of these lingering doubts, I would sometimes avoid hanging out with Rachel in certain situations. Every now and then I would grill her with questions or accuse her of manipulating situations in her favor so that she could attempt to start up a relationship with me again. If I thought that her secretly liking me was hurting her, I had no idea what kind of damage I was doing now. She deserved a better best friend than what I was giving her. I had lost all sight of appreciation for who she was, what she said, and how she treated me. Appreciation had been crushed into a million fragments, lost in the wind.

With this being said, the bad times came out from in between the better days. We shared countless good memories and times back then, but every now and then when this conversation flared up, it did nothing but hurt both parties. The friendship was subtly becoming a withering rope of trust, compassion, and attachment that would get untied a little more each time we argued about these issues. Little did I know someone was about to take a blowtorch to it.

In the fall of 2009, Rachel and I had lightly discussed getting back together. It was becoming obvious that we had started liking each other a little bit again and arguments about romantic feelings hurting our friendship had ceased. We had agreed that another "first date" was due and that I would be willing to give dating again a shot. To her dismay, and my shame, that never even happened. I changed my mind before a date even had a chance to spark and decided that this road was not one I wanted to travel again. I do not think a knife could have hurt her more than my decisions did that cold October.

Months later, she was vicariously introduced to one of my friends, who also denied the use of his name in this book, so we will call him Josh. They met in the beginning of 2010 and they quickly began finding an interest in each other. I pushed their advancements along because I cared for both of them, wanted both of them to be happy, and they both had expressed how much they wanted someone to call their own. I enjoyed seeing them together; these two friends of mine. I felt a little like Cupid, and felt a sense of pride in respect to their blossoming relationship. Oh, if only I had known.

Everything seemed to be okay except for Josh's slight apprehension about the past between Rachel and I. He got very antsy anytime someone would bring up our relationship or past things of that nature. Josh was very insecure about the whole thing, and he feared the stories about Rachel and I that the past may have been able to whisper in his ear. Even though it may have bothered him, everything was kept pretty reserved until one hot and sunny Oklahoma afternoon.

Rachel and Josh had been dating for several months by this time, and she and I had still been pretty close friends. My girlfriend at the time did not like my friendship with Rachel, and Josh was not too fond of Rachel and I hanging out together either. This just seemed like the age-old situation we had already been through before. I thoughtlessly went to her house one day to return a hard drive for her computer that I had borrowed, visited with her family a bit, went up to her room to chat for a second, and left. Nothing more, nothing less.

Josh and I shared talks previous to this incident and he explained some hesitation about her and I hanging out alone. He did not want us to be alone at any point, especially in a nostalgic setting such as her bedroom. As you read this you may agree with either his feelings or mine, but personally, this all seemed so alien to me seeing as how

I was the one who set them up to begin with. I was, in a way, being pushed away from one of my best friends. This did not settle too well with me. Josh knew there was history between Rachel and I ever since the times when we had dated and it had probably been brewing in his mind, building and building.

The next part of the story is an occurrence that I cannot help but wonder about. It mystifies me and wrinkles my brain to this day, and part of me cannot help but wonder if Rachel reacted this way solely because of my previous lack of appreciation for her. Later that afternoon, she texted me and told me that I would be getting hateful and aggressive texts from Josh a little bit later. She went on to explain that Josh was upset about me coming over unannounced to give her the flash drive back, and upset that I had gone to her bedroom. Then, she unleashed the bombshell.

Rachel proceeded to tell me that she was sorry for what was about to happen, but that she was going to fake "supporting" his decision to be mad at me for this. She asked me not to respond to any of these texts, and she said that she was going to immediately delete all of these texts from her phone. Then after Josh texted me, she was going to re-text me scolding me for what I had done earlier that day, and that she would be "taking his side" this time. She assured me that he would go through her phone at some point and that this was all very necessary. Rachel ended the texts saying that she did not think it should happen this way, but she just wanted to make sure he thought she agreed with him, and that she was very sorry. What? Was I dreaming? I wished so badly that I had been.

Sure enough, sometime afterward I received a plethora of hateful text messages from Josh, spelling out everything I had done wrong against him, as a friend and as an ex-boyfriend of Rachel's. He said he felt disrespected and that he did not want me near him or Rachel at all; a quick fix to their problems. He felt that what I had done was inexcusable and that he was done considering me as a friend. This wonderful event ended with him asking me to "please fuck off."

Rachel followed all of his texts messages up mirrored perfectly with what she had described earlier. She was scolding me for breaking their trust and told me that she was both hurt by and ashamed of me. She told me that maybe it was better if we were no longer fiends, and mentioned that I had really upset Josh. I could not help but sit in awe, rereading each text fifteen times, and think about everything that had happened between us that somehow lead us all to this day. Instantly, a haunting thought overtook me. I wished I had been a better friend to her through all the hearsay, opinions, and times we had shared before that day.

My thoughts instantly drifted to memories that I wished I could change between us. One of those memories framed one of those days when we had an argument about whether or not she still liked me. We were standing out by her Jeep, and as she was leaving I flat out told her that it only made it harder for us to be friends if she kept hanging on and hoping for another relationship. You could not even begin to stir the same emotion and hurt that I saw in her eyes that afternoon with one of those SPCA abused animal commercials. No matter if it was true or not that she still liked me on that day, I had dropped my appreciation for her. Now it was too late and I did not even have the chance to say I was sorry.

At the same time, all I could do is wonder how Rachel could have done such a flip-flop with this entire ordeal that was currently taking me for a ride. She even told me that she disagreed with him, but that she was going to "side with him" anyway for the sake of pleasing him. It angered, frustrated, hurt, saddened, confused, and worried me. Any other emotions I could think of that are involved in the death of a best-friendship?

Josh did not have to get as angry as he did, she could have stood up for me or our long-standing friendship, but things happened the way they happened regardless of how I felt. I wished to speak with them ever so badly in attempts to amend this whole thing. I did not want to lose either one of them as friends, but I had a haunting feeling that it was already too late; and for reasons I did not agree with.

The end of the summer brought him and I to the same social gathering at a mutual friend's house. This was the first time I had even been in the same area as him since before the day they texted me. He felt bad about everything and drunkenly pulled me out on the porch to talk everything out. We both apologized and he seemed to feel okay with everything, and we agreed to still carry out our plans to live together in our four-man room at college. Later that night, for the first time in months, I got a text from Rachel. It was weird getting a text like this from someone who was once my companion that I had practically grown up with, but who now was nothing but a stranger.

She asked for my help, but told me that she did not expect anything because of how she had treated me lately. I was informed that Josh was passed out cold from his alcohol intake in the middle of her driveway. He had drunk quite a bit that night, and she could not lift him herself. I immediately showed up and assisted her in getting him up. As I began lifting him, he woke up a bit and we got him back to our friend's house to sleep it off. That was the second-to-last time I would ever speak with Rachel in person again. She silently mouthed, "thank you so much." I nodded subtly, and as I turned to leave the house I told her, "You know I'd do it again too."

Things were awkward from then on. Josh and I moved into our dorm together at Oklahoma State along with two other friends of ours, as planned. I could tell he still did not want me talking with her, and I never had any idea how she felt. I talked with her a few times over Facebook, and all I could do was apologize and attempt to catch up with her. I felt remorse, and felt like I was slipping into quicksand and would never get the chance to set things right. She mentioned how she did not think we could ever be friends again because she was afraid of what may happen. There was an unexplainable amount of things that I wished I could just spill out and ask her. As time went on, communication came to a complete halt, and I moved across campus for my Residential Life job.

Months went by, and I would wonder about Rachel and Josh almost every day. I thought about it over time and came to a conclusion. I had to stand up for what I felt was right. I had to release a final extension of communication to her, let her know all my thoughts, and just hope for the best. My senior year of college was coming up, and I had no idea what the future held. There was a possibility I would never see either of them ever again, and I needed some sort of closure, no matter which way things went. I wrote up a lengthy letter and arranged to give it to her one day on campus.

As I nervously handed it to her, I told her that I hoped she could tell what I was trying to do with this letter. I remember the moment like it happened five seconds ago; that wondrously unsure look on her face as she took the letter from my hand. Just standing in front of her face-to-face felt weird. It was like I was witnessing an event straight from the history books. Little did I know that would probably be the last time I would ever see her or talk with her for the rest of my life.

The letter outlined everything I felt; all of my feelings about this situation, including those things I felt awful about. I elaborated on how I felt like I abused her availability as a friend of mine through those years, how sour I felt about how I handled our relationship when we had dated, and many other situations along the way. I also mentioned how I thought their relationship was the sole reason that I did not have the opportunity to talk with either of them anymore, and how much I wished things were different. I also bravely, but probably too boldly, mentioned how I felt like aspects of their relationship dragged them down in their own lives. All the shattered pieces of anything I had ever shared with Rachel were strewn about, and I was just trying to find them, pick them up, and glue it all back together.

A response came within hours, but not from Rachel; it was from Josh. Imagine that. It was the flash drive all over again. He sent me quite a few angry text messages that spelled out one plain and simple concept: if I spoke to either of them again, especially Rachel, he and I would "have a problem," as he put it.

I got my answer right then and there. He elaborated and went on to explain that him texting me spoke for them collectively, and that she had given him the letter to read. I had apparently really upset her with what I had written. He mentioned how poisonous he felt I was to both of their lives and how I did nothing but stir up drama and turmoil. It had all been said. It was done, and there was nothing else to be done, no matter how much I wanted things to change. I had held him as a good friend of mine. I had accepted her as one of my dearest and closest friends some time ago, and the one who knew me better than I may have ever even known myself. Now it was all gone.

I still wonder to this day if she has accepted everything I apologized for in that letter. I wonder if she feels okay with how everything turned out, or if the memories still haunt her like they do me. I wonder if he will ever desire to forgive or contact me. There are still so many things I wish I could say to her, and I just wish there was an opportunity to do so, but I digress. I have to let it rest eventually; they both made their decisions. I wonder how things may have turned out differently if I had been more appreciative to both of them in the days when we could have all shared a smile together; when no tears were shed and no fists were curled. Oh, what I would do to have that back.

We have to live life the right way the first time because once it happens, it is awfully hard to change and relive things. Many of the things that happen will not ever be able to be taken back; a crumpled paper will never be perfect again. My forlorn feelings about how I treated her will probably always stick with me, but I obviously cannot go back in time and change everything, especially with how things are now. So, I just have to learn from my frustration and live differently from now on; that is what we are all going to have to do, is it not?

I have a collection of picture books that grow with time as they get filled with memories of mine. Pictures, letters, notes, and other small items fill these pages and each item means something dear to me. I do not remember why she gave me this, but Rachel gave me a small card one day that she wanted me to keep handy for the rest of my life.

"If you can promise me one thing, <u>promise me</u> whenever you are sad, unsure, or you lose complete faith, that you'll try to see yourself **through <u>my eyes</u>**."
—Signed with her name.

I wonder how she sees me today through those same eyes; Josh, hard drive, that letter, our friendship, our past, how I treated her, and all.

This card is still in those memory books, and I read it ever so often. It always thrusts me back into countless memories, and that same forlorn feeling. I occasionally dream about having a simple conversation with either Rachel or Josh. I will be talking with them and just be thinking in awe, "Wow, it is actually happening!" I then wake up saddened to realize the truth that I am just dreaming.

I hope that "Josh" and "Rachel" read this book one day. Sadly, I do not think they will. Josh told a friend of mine that my book was a dumb idea and that I would probably never even finish it. And to them, I say this: no matter the situation, the time of day, the month, or the year, please never be afraid to contact me if you wish to do so. We have all done things in the past we are not too proud of, but I am here to say that if you ever care to speak with me again, I'll be willing to. If I am given the chance to be appreciative again, I will be sure to not strike out.

> "The deepest principle in human nature is the craving to be appreciated."
> —William James

The thing about this Pillar is that, with me at least, this is not the only example. I have several others in my life that come to mind when I think about having not appreciated someone enough while they were around. Several friends have left my life because of situations that I wish would have ended differently. One of those people that my heart yearns to see again, and tell her just how much I loved and appreciated her, is my grandmother. She was my mother's mom, and I called her Granny. She was, in so many ways, my second mother. Granny taught me a lot about sharing our lives with everyone we love and how to bless the world around us with love.

Our entire extended family fought a lot, and many members of my mom's family went through tough and trying times over the years. Granny was the one solid rock who everyone held onto. She gave them all common ground, and she kept the family glued together like no one else could ever dream of doing. After she passed away, the family split off and no one has been nearly as close as they were in the shadow of my grandma.

This lasting effect is just a single testament of the powerful and wonderfully-blessing life she led. Her smile, something that is still so easy and comforting for me to imagine about her, can instantly bring me a smile of my own, bring a quick tear to my eye, or quickly throw things back into perspective for me. Her influence and care for others was something to marvel, and everyone had days where they just stood in awe.

Growing up, I lived just two miles from my Granny and I saw her on a daily basis. She babysat me, cared for me when I was feeling less than perfect, entertained me those afternoons after elementary school, and played with me when I was over at her house. She always cut up fresh apple slices for me, gave me mulberries she had picked, or did anything to see me smile or give me some form of her affection. She always smiled and laughed with me, and my mom always told me that my Granny lived to enjoy and cherish everyone, and I was no exception. I put together so many puzzles with my Granny, and sometimes Grandpa would help too. We always cooked together in the late afternoons. Actually, I would just talk with her as she tried to teach me some of her secrets to her famous cooking the whole family loved so much. We shared so many little past times like that.

I was fifteen years old when my Granny passed away. I served as a pole bearer at her funeral, and I was so torn up inside. This was my second mother that raised me from birth who had just passed away, and I now had a part of my heart missing. She meant so much to me, but even on the day of her funeral, I started to realize that I could have shown how much I appreciated her so much better.

My thoughts drifted to times when my mom would tell me I needed to stop by and see Granny. She would tell me that Granny will not always be here with us, and I needed to take the time and make sure to see her. I wished I had not only listened to my mother more often, but that I had desired to visit Granny more on my own accord. Time is priceless, and irreversible.

She was in and out of the hospital for several conditions she faced as she neared the end of her wonderful time here on Earth. Everyone who was lucky enough to be able to laugh and smile with her knows how precious she was and made sure they visited her a lot in those days. I knew the time neared in those few years, but as a thirteen-and-fourteen-year-old boy, I did not dwell on those kinds of thoughts too often. I visited her frequently, but I realized later just how much more I could have done for her; a quality-over-quantity kind of situation.

One of my last memories that I hold of her, and one I still cherish dearly, is visiting her on one of her last days. As she lay in her own bed in the house she had raised my mother in, I walked in to visit her and knew it may be the last time that I ever got to speak with her. She was very tired and I was nervous about what to say or do. She wearily glanced over to see her young grandson and just cracked a big smile. A memory that still brings a smile to my face.

She reached out to hold my hand, which I held gently, and I talked with her for a little bit as she weakly laid there. She reminded me of how I used to sing to her at night before she laid me down at night, talked about how much I loved our puzzles, my Hot Wheels, and all my dinosaurs, and how much she loved having me around. All I could do was hold onto her hand, attempt to hold a quivering smile, and cry quietly as she drifted off to sleep. She was very tired.

The thoughts on my lack of appreciation set in when I think about her final years she shared with all of us. I was only one of her twenty-three grandchildren, but I still felt such a close connection with her; she had that much compassion to give out. I may have lived nearby and I may have been able to see her more often than most, but she loved all of us immensely with all of herself. I wish I had spent more time at her side, giving her just a fraction of the love she shared with me as I grew up under her wing.

I realize that I should not beat myself up about how I acted back then, but I still wish I could have told her once more how much of a blessing she was to have had in my life. I cry every time I visit her grave and can't help but think about how wonderful and genuine she was. She inspired who I have tried to become and I yearn so much to be like her. She touched my life and spirit and will always be with me.

I miss her and wish I could speak with her one more time; hold her hand and give her a hug. I wish I could tell her how much her now-older grandson appreciated her, loved her, and how much he feels like he took her for granted when he was an adolescent. *I'm sorry* probably are not the right words, but *thank you* probably are. I love you, Granny.

> "Appreciation is a wonderful thing: It makes what is excellent in others belong to us as well"
>
> —Voltaire

Who do you have in your life that deserves appreciation? What if today was their last day to live and tomorrow would already be too late to say anything to them again? How would you feel, and what would you try to tell yourself as that heavy ball hung in your throat? We all have those people and things in life that we absolutely love. We all have things we will miss someday, and for the sake of all things timely, take the time to appreciate what you have today; before it is way too late.

Appreciation can be shown in so many ways. That is what makes it so beautiful. Everyone expresses themselves differently, and people cherish different aspects of life in various ways. Tell those people out there how much good they do for you and your life. Let them know why you love to see them; why they make you smile. If we lived with each other as if it may be the last time we see each other, then we could live without the fear of tomorrow. You would know that your loved ones knew how you felt, and there would not be any questions or doubts. As they say, you never know when.

Tell that someone why you love them, and share it with them often. Give that cute dog of yours an extra-long walk. Tell your kids why you find them to be the best ever. Give that friend of yours a big hug, no matter who is around. Let us be timely in our expressions, and let us be sincere.

We want to let those who deserve to be a part of our lives know how much they matter to us. Taking things for granted, especially those close to our hearts and souls, is a dangerous game. There is a time limit to this game, and no one knows when the timer is going to go off. Maybe we will just have to play as hard as we can the entire time and live our lives in a way that will keep our hindsight from ever coming to haunt us.

Maintain Time for Yourself

Stress is just another part of our daily equations. I think we can all agree on that. It is a common word we all use, complain about, and try to resist from dusk until dawn. Stress has been scientifically proven to both physically and mentally harm us over time. Because of this, I find it to be something we should be weary of, observe, and act upon accordingly. We can get to certain points in our lives where we feel like so much is expected of us, and sometimes we can stretch ourselves too thin. Way too thin. Just like we sleep every night, we need periods of recharging to be able to function and make it through another day. This stress our minds and body deals with is no different.

This theme rises out of a significant period of time in my life that I did not know I would ever experience. I was twenty years old, busy and as stressed as ever. I had been through a lot of different situations in the past few months and I felt lost. I needed help, and there was one major reason that I had backed myself into this corner. I had left no time for myself; none at all. I visited with my Residential Life supervisor and excellent friend, Heather, about my situation and she had a personal suggestion for me: on-campus counseling.

"Beware the bareness of a busy life."

—Socrates

Like many others, I had always associated counseling with people who were dealing with great amounts of grief, or people who were severely troubled inside their crumbling or bruised lives. I did not feel like this was my case, at all. I did not want to have to go to a counselor. Why would I think I needed help from someone like that? I felt like I needed to have some serious problems or that I needed to suffer from some traumatic experience to require counseling of any kind. Heather's recommendation was almost embarrassing for me at the time, and it was difficult for me to even approach the idea of needing counseling.

I appreciated Heather's suggestion and told her I would give it some thought. I walked out of her office holding a student counseling services card, not knowing what I was going to do. This was a weird feeling for someone who always just heard about counseling in movies or who just heard about others getting counseling for traumatic events. I sat that card on my desk and looked at it every day. I did not feel comfortable saying that I needed help through counseling. I thought on it more and more, and eventually decided something.

I eventually decided that I should not fear needing help and guidance from someone. I started feeling like it should not be an issue of pride, and that it should not matter whether or not I felt weird about receiving help. I had to be willing to accept the fact that I needed help with how my moods and my anxiety seemed to be imploding on me, and from those who knew what they were doing. There was no reason for embarrassment. I just needed some help from professional and patient individuals. These were people who would be there for me.

I signed up and used a recommendation from Heather about who I could request as my counselor, and we set up a first meeting time after my preliminary check-in with the office. The campus supplied five free visits to any student or faculty, and I had every intention of using all five. The whole process was so awkward and uncomfortable for me at first, but the idea of something new like professional counseling was somewhat exciting. Perhaps this was just because of the unpredictability it offered. I found myself getting anxious and ready for my first session as the appointment neared.

My feelings revealed something to me: I had needed someone to vent to, to share my problems with, and to help me along. Someone who was different than what I already had in my life. I was stressed, constantly frustrated, and upset with myself. These professionals were really going to listen; they would be there for me. It was so evident when I talked with my counselor for the first time that he truly wanted to help me get through this stressful and unnerving time in my life. This guy was so empathetic, and he hardly knew me. I guess that is why he got paid to do this; because he was so good at it.

My first session flew by. I was pouring out information and ranting at ninety miles an hour. I felt myself feeling better as I just kept burning through old subjects. I was already feeling relief wash over me after letting go of some of these pent-up emotions. We covered everything you could think of, at least a little bit, in that first hour; the first session. He and I both saw that this was obviously good for me, and I was ready for the next week's session. I just felt like he cared a lot and he was there to listen. Truly listening is such a valuable thing to do for someone. Just saying.

During one of the five counseling sessions, we started talking about my stress and how lost I had been feeling recently. He had me talk about everything and try to figure out what all this stress was stemming from. He could tell how busy I was and asked me a single question. "When was the last time you did something refreshing for yourself?" I thought about it for a while. I could not recall. He then used a wonderful metaphor that I have used countless times since then to describe this situation to others. He told me that I had no water left in my glass.

I was confused, at first. He went on to explain his metaphor. We all have our daily time we use in our lives, which is also coupled with our emotional energy that we can share with others. This represents our glass. That glass is filled with water, and every time we do something, or get involved with anything we pour some water out. Around this time, I had a lot of things on my plate at once. I was stretched very thin both mentally and emotionally. There were a lot of different situations going on in my life, each requiring some of the water in my glass to be poured out. Now that my glass had gone dry, I had no water left to pour for myself.

> "A poor life this is, full of care, if we have no time to stand and stare."
>
> —William Henry Davies

He advised several ways to allow myself to start filling my glass back up. I needed to learn to gauge my stress and anxiety levels, and I also needed to find time to do things that let me unravel. He knew I liked journaling about my life, so he advised creating certain time blocks every day for doing just that. He knew I liked going to the gym and working out, and he said I should not skip such activities. Hitting the gym released some of that negative energy and there was more to these activities than I probably even knew of. I loved catching up with friends, watching my favorite movies, listening to my favorite bands while (horribly) singing along in the car, and other simple pleasures. These small escapes were my own miniature mental vacations.

Once I realized that I needed to save some personal time for myself, and how grateful I should be, each day was a whole new story. I dealt with a lot in the following months, that I normally would have found stressful, but I fended it off with ease thanks to my new state of mind. Finding a little time for myself to journal, constantly listening to music I loved, hitting the gym, watching good movies, and truly taking the time out to enjoy quality time with friends changed my daily life. It changed my mood, and lent me some water back. I finally had some water that I could pour out if I needed to do so.

This metaphor works so well once we start living it. Take heed and notice how energized and refreshed you feel after an escape from the routine grind. Perhaps we just need a new perspective? Or maybe we just need a break for ourselves. Take five, everyone.

I did not get to take many vacations as a kid because we never really had the money. I got the chance this year to spend my Spring Break in the beach town of Gulf Shores, Alabama. I was so excited for my getaway opportunity. My mom and I were going to see family while down there, and I also brought four friends along for the experience. I got to witness the beach for the second time in my life and I got to travel and get away from everything for five days. Unplugging and soaking in everything became an unbelievably reviving experience.

Thanks to some family connections, we got to stay in a condo on the beachside for an amazing bargain. When I first laid my eyes on the condo the overwhelming amounts of relief, emotion, and sheer happiness I was fortunate enough to be experiencing brought immediate tears to my eyes. It was so nice to get away, and be here in a beautiful condo by the beach; a first for me. It was very surreal to be able to just relax and forget about all the troubles of our lives for a few days; to recharge our batteries.

> "Take rest; a field that has rested gives a bountiful crop."
>
> —Ovid

Often times while in our moments of escape, during the times we truly get to unplug and relax, we begin to see how much we do not have to worry about. We begin to see a new light on old issues and realize we worry too much. Sometimes we discover that a new mindset could change our stress levels all together. If we bring in a deep breath, take a step back, and look at everything for a second, we could possibly reap much more benefit than we may think. We just may save ourselves.

When I got back home from Gulf Shores, something occurred to me: I was able to do the same workload as I had been doing before we left for Spring Break, but did not feel the same amounts of pressure or anxiety. It was such a breath of fresh air for my mentality, and it was ever so welcomed. It was amazing to get to see the differences of a clear and refreshed mind first-hand. It spoke volumes about this principle. It truly works.

Do you enjoy some time for yourself often enough? Do those around you need some time away? Do they need to be unplugged?

These are all questions to take away from this chapter. If we have enough time for ourselves, could we help others? If we do not, then what can we do to improve our situations? Finding our little escapes can become priceless. It can be so rejuvenating to get away in the midst of those trying and difficult times. The mental refreshment can be just like a cold glass of water on a hot summer day.

But not an empty one, right?

Apathy Is Dangerous

Apathy is a word I learned in middle school and immediately liked for some reason. I heard it while listening to some of my favorite musicians at the time and thought it sounded cool. Later on in college, I would come to know its definition by heart and would realize how dangerous I thought it was. Its potential to suffocate people from their own opinions is very scary to me, and it is something that I think is dangerous not only to our generation, but to our country. I feel like people need to know what they stand for and care about it; a lot.

People who do not care about anything, or who do not live for certain beliefs or aspirations in life do not really have much to live for. As human beings, our cares drape over us like a lion's mane. In the face of indifference, our mane becomes mere decoration and our potential passion and life inside us becomes a dried-up fallacy. A person who does not care about anything lacks personality. People who are apathetic about things in life can seem lazy, rude, or possibly even unsympathetic. It all depends on how you see it, and how they see you. Essentially, in a world as chaotic and ever-changing as ours, it can become quite dangerous; especially on a mass level.

I have always tried not to be apathetic for as long as I can remember. I always felt like it was well worth it to care about things, speak my mind when asked to do so, and stand for things I took to heart and mind. Of course, this has evolved over time in my life, and it has swelled in importance. Most of the evolution in my opinions about apathy has come from my time spent at OSU. I have seen a lot of apathy, most of it dangerously subtle, at a place I figured I would not: at a state university. It bothers me, and I wish it were different sometimes; a lot of the time.

> "My generation's apathy. I'm disgusted with it. I'm disgusted with my own apathy too, for being spineless and not always standing up against racism, sexism and all those other—isms the counterculture has been whining about for years."
>
> —Kurt Cobain

I have only lived what I expect to be merely a portion of my life, and I have experienced enough interactions with others to figure out that apathy bothers me. It exists everywhere. These examples I will share with you are relevant to me still, and I use them as stories when I speak about this issue with other people. One could say that the fact I care about this issue enough to speak on it, and write such a chapter in this book, shows my stance on the relevance of the issue. What gives you reason to not be apathetic, and makes your skin crawl; makes your blood boil? What triggers that mane of yours to stand on end?

A part of not being apathetic is cracking yourself open. This makes many of us feel very vulnerable and susceptible to the attacks of others. But this shows others what we feel, think, and what bothers us; the intimate worries that keep us up at night. This can be flat-out scary sometimes. It can be hard for us to migrate out of an apathetic state of mind. After all, if we do not care about this type of thing in the first place, why change anything? That is the danger in it. It is hard to escape once you let it creep in. It turns a blind eye to others and can speak volumes about our personality. But then again, why would we care in the first place if we were apathy-ridden?

My first story is one that frustrated me. During the spring semester of my junior year at OSU, I had a Consumer Behavior class. It was a marketing class focused on the mindset and psychology involved in consumer products and what drives economies. My professor was one of my favorites that I have ever had, because of how much he cared for the class and the issues at hand. He frequently used current events to bring across a point or to emulate what he was trying to teach us. Things became emotional several times in class while talking about troubling situations that surround us in today's world. He was a very passionate man, and I respected and admired him for it.

One of these issues involved the Dove Campaign. For those that do not know, the Dove Campaign is a movement started to spread the word about the air brushing in pictures of models and celebrities in magazines and other print material. The campaign is also passing a focus of confidence to those young girls and women out there who feel down on themselves because of society's pressures.

This issue has started to affect the lives of individuals, especially younger children who strive to find acceptance and self-worth in the young and crucial time of their lives. They look at pictures of perfectly-sculpted, thin men and women, and compare these altered and fake pictures to themselves. Suicide rates of young girls and self-esteem figures represented by many polled women all over the nation show the effect this supposed harmless airbrushing has on others.

People in the industry who support this practice defend that people should understand and realize that the images are airbrushed, and that it is not real. Of course, we would not want anything to cut into their profits. They defend that we should understand why they do it, and let our young children know this as well. The Dove Campaign focuses on using natural beauty as a source of empowerment and confidence for both children and adults. They want to stress to people the dangerous effects of this image-altering process and possibly get something initiated to limit it and its effects. I believe in it and find it admirable, but that is merely my own opinion.

My professor was talking about these issues, and showing us videos that the campaign had made to show the stark difference between real images and those that were airbrushed and completely altered. It was breathtaking and sad to think that little girls out there would strive to look like this, even though it was not real.

Children would never even have the chance to know the difference though. "Seven out of ten girls think they are not good enough," according to one of the articles from their website. My professor was elaborating on the cause, and you could tell this is something that had affected people he knew. Anyone could hear the emotion in his voice and infer how much he cared about this kind of topic.

He opened up the floor for discussion. He asked an auditorium-sized room filled with around one hundred college students, about half of them women, what they think about all this. Crickets. I am just staring at the professor, thinking about all of this in my head, and I look around. I saw at least ten people in front of me on their laptops. They were navigating Facebook and looking through sports websites. My professor tried to push along the discussion and it moved for a little while due to me and a few people in the front, but that was about it.

I wished that more people in there had been as affected as I was. I wished they cared enough to let it bother them; for them to feel emotions for those affected and formulate an opinion about it for themselves. Typical lectures do not focus on real-world issues that are affecting each and every one of us day in and day out, but it did not seem to matter to them. Incredulous, it really is, how little people can care about things as they sit in a classroom that they paid a lot of money to attend.

> "Science may have found a cure for most evils; but it has found no remedy for the worst of them all—the apathy of human beings."
>
> —Helen Keller

Besides that class, there were other situations that elicited the same feeling for me. We had a day of silence for human trafficking on campus. They were selling yellow shirts for students to wear that day, and I figured the campus would be swarming with yellow shirts from people hoping to spread awareness and show support. On the day of silence there were only a few yellow shirts here and there. It let me down. But then again, I was no different. I did not buy a shirt because I had a job interview that day, and was wearing a suit to all of my classes and meetings. Regardless, I had wished that campus would have been swimming in yellow.

I have watched apathy affect people around me that I have, in a way, grown up with. It haunts their lives, even if they never admit it. I have seen relationships around me crumble because of apathy. Depression and anxiety spring out of the darkness in the absence of true passion and direction. I have witnessed it sour their moods and infect their healthy motivation they once carried. Friends have told me that they felt useless, lost, or even worthless at times. Their passion and emotions grow dim; their fire starts burning out. Who would relight it if it were to go out?

I wish the best for them and try to speak with some of them about their attitudes. Some are quite receptive, and we have excellent talks about it that lead somewhere. Some of them refuse that their attitude is any different than mine. I do not demean or look down on them, but I just want them to share those great joys in life: passion, excitement, motivation, joy, and countless other benefits from a life relinquished from apathy. Keep your personal fires burning. Throw some gas on it and watch it grow.

When you watch the news, see a horrible story in the paper, or hear of a tragedy that happened somewhere in the world, do you find yourself caring? Does it make you want to do something? Or perhaps you shrug it off and snicker to yourself that you are sure glad that did not happen to you. It is understood that we cannot do anything about a lot of the situations and occurrences that we hear about in life, but if the feelings and natural compassion exists, then the potential for action is beautiful.

If we harbor the care and yearning to help others, then we can act upon it in those certain situations when we are actually able to help out. Those crucial moments, when our lack of disregard is supposed to shine, speak immense volumes about who we are, what we have become, and how we view life. Our mane shines bright under the African sun.

"The death of democracy is not likely to be an assassination from ambush. It will be a slow extinction from apathy, indifference, and undernourishment."
—Robert M. Hutchins

Another situation that instantly leads me to think about this Pillar, in reference to my time at OSU, is the infamous group project assignment. We all know those group members who sit at the table with everyone else, but have an indescribable look on their face. I feel like they would rather have their arms twisted off than have to work on this project with the rest of us. It is a very frustrating feeling to pour your brain and strife into certain projects, but others just ride your grade and stare at you from behind their apathetic cell. I cannot help but think to myself *what would it take to see these same people overjoyed and consumed in excitement?* Why are they so miserable when they paid thousands to be there?

To an extent, what we take personally becomes what we stand for. If your heart sinks when you hear or see things that bother you, then you are probably not a zombie; a drone of the current corporate world. When we get that feeling, we know it inside ourselves. If we do not take anything to heart and live impersonal lives, then what joy or silver lining is there to life? What do we have to look forward to, to get excited for, or to stand up for if we do not care about such things? To not be detached and share yourself with the world, in a way, is to show who you are; to be a real living-and-breathing human being with passions, desires, and values.

Having patience with other people is needed, but we must all take a stand for something. Sometimes I need to realize that, like me, people may have deeply-seeded concerns for the world around them but may not get to act on it too often. I have thought about starting to make short films about certain social and worldly issues. Maybe I could make a difference. How could you make a difference? How could you open up and show how much you care about the passions in your life?

We should all care about the world around us. Everyone dies, but only some people live. Only some people *truly* live. To fight for others and love is to live, and apathy does not coincide with those things very well. It is poisonous and very lonely. Do not let indifference take away your vigor, your soul, or your personality. Do not let it strip the lion's mane from your neck. I ask you on behalf of the rest of the world: please do not be apathetic. Please care.

Perhaps together, we can all take it one step further. Maybe we can also start acting on our concerns. We could end up changing the world one voice at a time, shaking our manes a bit, and jolting the world with our roars.

KEEP RESPONSIBILITY

Walking down the beach, footsteps trailing you for miles, being lapped by the soft waves of the ocean. Sound a bit like the way our impact on this Earth works? Not quite. How about trekking through an entire freshly paved parking lot, with each footstep forever engraving and impressing on the landscape? That is what each and every one of our impacts here on Earth looks more like.

Responsibility stems from several different topics, but they all shape one central issue: that everything we do has lasting effects. From social to environmental, it is futile to think we can do what we want for years and never leave a wake. You know how choppy a lake gets on Memorial Day weekend. That is life, in itself, in the midst of all our splashing around.

The bigger of a life you lead and the bigger of a boat you drive, the more wake and turbulence you have the potential to create. The more each one of us does, the more responsible we are going to have to be as we prance about in life. Create the right kind of wake behind you with that huge boat of yours, jet-skis from all over will be flocking to your six o' clock.

> "You cannot escape the responsibility of tomorrow by evading it today."
> —Abraham Lincoln

So, how is it that we can strive to be more responsible? First, let us consider the environment. Here is a mental picture that leads me to really start taking this idea into consideration. The next time you throw away an item or drive somewhere, multiply your impact by six billion. Yeah, six billion. If everyone carelessly threw away a pop bottle at the same time you did, there went over millions of cubic space from our Earth that we will never get back. Now, remind me, how many of those do we throw away in a year's time?

As you can see, our environmental impact takes off incredibly quickly if we apply what we are doing to the rest of the world. Regardless of whether people believe in global warming or not, it is obvious that our environment is coming into a crucial time of make or break. We are going to have to start doing things to curb what is currently happening if the Earth is to be as beautiful tomorrow as it is today. Visit your local landfill. It will make you sick.

In one of my classes (Brand Marketing, to be exact), we were discussing the environmental impacts our waste is having on this particular area in the middle of the Pacific Ocean. This area includes a few islands known by the name of the Midway Islands and a certain species of bird called the Laysan Albatross. The conversation evolved into a hypothetical discussion about what we would do if we were the company owners of BIC.

BIC is a manufacturer of disposable lighters, and there had been a lot of recent news stories about disposable lighters and how they are becoming a large hazard to the Laysan Albatross population on the islands. The adult birds were picking up these lighters drifting in the ocean and would fly them back to give to their offspring as food. The birds thought that they were carrying back legitimate food items, and they could easily spot the lighters in the ocean because of their shiny components. Young and adult birds alike were dying from these events.

Our professor asked us what we thought of the press coverage, the effects on these birds that were dying from our trash, and what to do with the business products. A girl in front instantly spoke up: "That's bad PR. It just makes you look bad." Then I heard a guy behind me quietly remark, "Who even cares?" The girl next to him replied, "I don't know. Nobody even lives there." I almost turned around to see if they had been joking or not.

Of course. No humans live there, and we do not need these birds to be able to drive to the mall or the theater on the weekends. Why else would we need to care about such a situation? So many of us can get into a mindset that traps us from caring about anything that does not directly intersect with our lives. People are not able to care about the environment if they cannot grasp the ultimate impact it eventually has.

There could have been a plethora of responses better than the first three that I immediately picked up on, but that is just my opinion. I could not help but instantly think about how frustrated situations like these make me feel. Animals die every day because of some waste we throw on the ground, regardless of who cares or what they think. It does nothing but smear the beautiful painting the world is trying to craft for us.

> "The price of greatness is responsibility."
> —Winston Churchill

I am not requesting that tomorrow we all become executive members of the green party and citizen's arrest anyone who litters in our presence. But I do think that a step in a more responsible direction would not only help the world around us while we share it these years we are alive, but for the many years and generations to come. From recycling more, to throwing less away, there are thousands of ways we can pitch in to the movement. If we can walk down the beach, leaving footprints behind that are able to be swept away by natural swipes of the ocean, we could keep from scarring the landscape as we progress along.

In terms of responsibility, moving from consumerism to sustainability is just a single note we could play on an entire spectrum of disciplines. From the mistakes we make, to the trustworthiness that comes with the promises we make to others, there are a lot of elements that can mix in together, like the paint on a paintbrush. One of those issues I find increasingly important as we all get older is the issue of accountability. If the stilts we walk around on did not splinter and break as we trek through the dirt, maybe we could get where we needed to be going.

The more often we hold ourselves accountable, the quicker we learn to be responsible in all facets. Putting ourselves in leadership positions, taking on tasks that others depend on you for, and following through on personal goals can cultivate this sense of personal responsibility. In a sense, it teaches us to be trustworthy, dependable, people of our word.

As the amount that we do on a daily basis grows, the more we have to keep responsibility with us at all times. The bigger a boat is, the bigger its wake. The more power and authority we begin to carry in our lives, at school, or in our career, the more responsibility we will need to possess. People depend on others socially, emotionally, and sometimes even vitally. It is impossible to predict or to know when this mentality will come in handy or when we will need it to hold us up in the quicksand of time.

During my time here at OSU, I have found that there is one professor in particular everyone could never help but remember. Some resent him, while others praise him as the best professor they ever had or the best thing to happen to the Entrepreneurship Department at Oklahoma State. His name is Dr. Morris, and he makes you take responsibility, whether you want it or not.

On the first day of class, I was scared absolutely senseless. Never before had I experienced a professor who booms and commands a classroom like he does. Eye contact that could break bones and a voice that ripples skin accompanies his very sharp attitude and expectations of students. Combined, you have a strong potential for memorable moments in the classroom.

Some say he is an absolute jerk because of the way he handles interactions with students. He can raise his voice rather quickly or say things that seem very abrasive, seemingly out of nowhere. He can seem pretty condescending; sometimes people feel like he would do anything to be able to pick at your worst fears in life, like a pit-bull going for the jugular.

Others would say that he is the most inspiring and moving professor because of his expectations of students, devotion to teaching, and belief that students come first, no matter what. He is an excellent teacher and knows exactly how to get you to relate to and learn new concepts quickly. He is incredibly passionate and driven to be an excellent instructor. Not only that, but he has been the main driving force that has taken the new School of Entrepreneurship here at OSU from brand new to one of the best in the country, all in under three years. He is a man of results.

One of the things that set Dr. Morris apart from many other professors is how much he holds you accountable. If you mess up and do not do an assignment that you should have done, be ready for public humiliation and a drill-instructor-worthy chewing about how you are wasting everyone's time. He expects a lot out of his students. Being on both sides of the situation, being yelled at and seeing others take the heat, I decided something: he expects so much out of people because he feels that is what the norm should be. I cannot help but agree.

> "When a man points a finger at someone else, he should remember that four of his fingers are pointing at himself."
>
> —Louis Nizer

I once heard Dr. Morris say to us, "You know, for once I would like to be impressed by the effort put forth by a student. Is that too much for me to ask?" Whether through the fear of the harshest reprimand academically possible or the sincere urge to impress and excel for internal reasons, Dr. Morris knows how to get students to do their work and do it correctly. He gets people motivated no matter the incentive, to not only do the minimum possible, but to do what is expected of them. We were frequently told that, by the age of twenty and twenty-one, we should all be masters in something-now was the time to show it.

Some professors extend deadlines for a whiny class. Others stammer around when people do not respond to their discussion questions. Not Dr. Morris. One day in our class, a team was presenting a case analysis and action plan. It was obvious from the beginning that they were not well prepared, and that they did not follow his instructions on how to present. He stopped them early on, telling the class that "this is what it looks like to have a complete and total disregard for the class and for other students' time." Class was dismissed right there, and he walked out. Later, the team was given a second chance to try and salvage their grade, but his actions their first time around spoke volumes to the team.

Many people do not like him because of his attitude or because of his high expectations. Dr. Morris can sometimes intimidate me to a shiver, and he can be a little quick to anger with people. But one thing remains true about him: he holds others accountable and gives them a fair chance to prove themselves. I had an internship with the School of Entrepreneurship and had frequent interactions with him. The interns that did not do what was expected got yelled at. Meetings could turn awkward and uncomfortable really quickly. But getting a handshake from Dr. Morris and being told, "Good work, Ivan," at the end of the semester placed a feeling of accomplishment within me that no other professor has ever been able to give me.

I think that there is a mentality that can creep into many people's lives that says *oh, it's okay. I can skate by.* If we do not take ourselves and what we do seriously, and what we do, then how can we expect others to do the same? If we let others down enough, the old *fool me twice, shame on me* rule is exactly what they will think. In life, we are all building human pyramids so that we can all get through the days together. Let other people fall enough, and they won't include you in their pyramid anymore.

The kind of behavior that chains us to our effects on the world around us has to come from within. People may be able to help you out by giving you tasks and holding you accountable, but when it comes down to it, responsibility is going to have to be a job done all by ourselves. No one walks anywhere without leaving some sort of mark. From dirt to snow, our impressions trail behind us from birth. How are you going to shape your footprints of tomorrow?

STAY HUMBLE

Throughout history, many thinkers and philosophers tended to stress the importance of humility. Today, this Pillar seems a little lost in the midst of all the flaming opinions zipping around everywhere. Pride and self-love frequently tend to take some sort of priority over humility here in America, especially within our generation. Research studies have proven that as time goes on the rates of clinically-sociopathic behavior continuously increases in the United States, especially among younger individuals. That is severely unsettling to me; maybe even bone-chilling.

Staying humble, like several of the other Pillars, ties into being somewhat selfless. As we meander through life, we must keep several things in mind. We have to remember, in our most glorious moments, that there will always be someone doing as well or better than ourselves. It may be in some completely different category or in some way that you may not even think is impressive. But then again, glory and pride is all perspective.

We also need to keep in mind that if it were not for every single person around us in our lives, we would not be anywhere close to where we are today. In a way, staying humble is reminding ourselves that we could never truly do everything in life completely on our own; period.

> "A man wrapped up in himself makes a very small bundle."
>
> —Benjamin Franklin

My mom attempted to instill a sense of terminal humility in me as she raised me, her only child. She always tried to get me to remember that I am not better than anyone else and that arrogance is a closed-off road leading to nothing but a cliff. She wanted me to know that anytime we think we are better than another person, it is only because of how we perceive things; how it is only in the eye of the beholder. To treat others how we would want to be treated, and give them the respect we would also like to receive, is a priceless way to bless the lives of others around you.

The town of Owasso, in Northeastern Oklahoma, is my hometown where I was born and raised. For me, Owasso brings this Pillar to mind. In order for me to elaborate on how it ties into the Pillar, we first have to take a look at a few things. Owasso is a suburb of Tulsa, Oklahoma. It is in a unique situation, and like some of the other suburbs of Tulsa, it defies the norm of what some would consider "Oklahoma towns." In a way, the whole town is an isolated and unique area.

Many people in the New England area or out on the West Coast probably think that all Oklahomans drive big trucks and we all wear cowboy hats. I have even heard of those who think the classic "cowboys and Indians" still happens in Oklahoma today. There are many people in Oklahoma that do wear hats and drive trucks, but a generalization like that would be incredibly inaccurate. Especially in Owasso, and other suburbs of Tulsa like Broken Arrow and Jenks, the typical rural-cowboy image of citizens is very far from the truth. People tend to generalize other places when they do not know very much about them, and it can have lasting negative effects.

Going to high school in Owasso was my biggest personal experience that confronted me with this issue while growing up. As I grew from kindergarten to college, I went through many changes over the years; some of those years being a little less glamorous than others. I was never the popular kid, or the most handsome guy in school, and I was one of those kids who was quiet and considered weird or nerdy. People probably thought of me as that kid who was just there, but you probably did not know how I got there, or how

I left. With this being said, it was probably pretty easy for me to get agitated at others' behavior.

As life went on and we all got older, humility and lack thereof became a more noticeable character trait. It would be a generalized exaggeration to say that the youth of Owasso was arrogant, which would be a mistake. Instead, I would just say that some of the individuals that took residence in my hometown had an arrogant way about themselves, and it became quite noticeable. Some people from Owasso would like to consider it somewhat of an upper-class area. Many people that worked in the large city of Tulsa resided in the nice neighborhoods of Owasso. Many kids thought they were far better than those surrounding them, and in all sorts of ways.

> "You shouldn't gloat about anything you've done; you
> ought to keep going and find something better to do."
> —David Packard

My first car cost my family $1,200, and I was pretty happy with it. I drove up to school each morning, squeaky suspension and all, and parked my car next to the rest of my friends' cars. I was just happy to be driving. Then I saw kids drive up to school in BMWs, Mercedes, Escalades, and brand new cars. Some of these kids would have their chin in the air as if their necks were permanently cricked like that, and they would stare at everyone as if they were peasants begging for table scraps. Then they would proceed to walk into school as if they were about to enter the ring at a WWE wrestling event. They may have been nice and genuine inside, but if so, it was not shining through at the time.

These people who acted like WWE character The Rock on a daily basis carried a certain sense of arrogance with them into the classroom as they acted like the others kids were lucky to be in the same room as them. It is a high school sort of thing, and everyone knows those kids throughout childhood who had not ever heard about the concept of humility. However, this was increasingly obvious to me, being someone who resented the very mindset and behavior to its core. Maybe it stemmed from envy? These people made me feel put down and like I was nobody. We all know how that feeling burns as it shivers through our innards. What if these certain kids were able to see how they looked in the eyes of those around them? Would things change?

Kids would poke fun or pick fights with kids who were not considered "popular." Some of these kids who felt like they were social saints would always brag about themselves, their families, or their money; and the more who could hear it, the better. Not to mention, the majority of their stories were probably just tall tales fabricated to impress their self-constructed audiences. Owasso was the age-old stereotypical situation of the jocks, the bullies, the nerds, and so on. Just because it was a stereotype did not make it any more acceptable. The attitudes of kids who walk on the feelings, liberties, and opinions of others do nothing but inflict pain and spread dissent.

Witnessing behavior from teenagers like these would make you wonder where they got their behavior and mentality from. Then you would look around and notice many adults, probably some of their parents, acting the exact same way. Some of these people acted as if it were a shame they even had to be out in public areas with all these other people. Do not get me wrong though. This is not just happening in Owasso. It is happening everywhere. From California to New York, from New York to Australia, we have all witnessed it.

Let me give a quick example that I think emulates this Pillar perfectly. At the Coachella Music Festival of 2011, an increasingly-popular British folk rock group by the name of Mumford and Sons played for the biggest audience that they had ever performed in front of. Before leaving the stage after their set, they were nearly in tears because of how grateful they were of all the cheering fans. They usually did not play events that large, and the support that they received overwhelmed them. Their sincerity was overflowing. Immediately after, Kanye West drops down from the ceiling on a chariot and graces us with a giant forty-foot statue of himself. Below him and his statue, were people placed on stage who then began worshiping him. I feel a breeze of difference blowing through the window here.

I feel like this is a Pillar that some people may find silly or redundant. Our society seems to bat away humility, and yell that it is for the meek and shy. We are taught from the days as toddlers to smear victory in competitors' faces, brag about our abilities, and walk around like we own the place. Just take a look at the average grade-school boy's t-shirt. If it has writing on it, there will likely be a sarcastic saying about being an awesome winner or how cool they are. Sure, it is just young children's clothing, but where does the line get drawn?

At what point do we admit that arrogance, self-pride, or 'showboating" starts rubbing off on us? From television to magazines, flashy and overly proud behavior is the norm and seems to be the expected demeanor of an entire nation. In a world where top-forty songs do nothing but brag about how much money they make or how much cooler than you they are, and where people scoff at others who do not wear clothes as fancy or drive cars as luxurious as them, I have to ask: when did cockiness become a personality trait instead of a flaw?

> "None are so empty as those who are full of themselves."
>
> —Benjamin Whichcote

I have always treated this situation with frustration that borders on the edge of anger. Situations saturated with arrogance bother me and lead me to wish nothing but for things to be different. I can only hope that these people will see the world differently someday, and that they will look back on certain situations in life with embarrassment. With that being said, I was having a talk with a friend of mine, the same one from *Empathy Not Envy*, which lent me a new perspective. She said that she felt sorry for arrogant and egotistical people. She was convinced that it is always just a cover, and that the people who are actually comfortable with themselves do not have to act outward about it. She felt sorry for them because she felt like it was their cry for help in an oddly round-about way.

Later that evening I could not help but dwell on this new concept, and a certain friend of mine came to mind. I felt like this friend carried an arrogant attitude with them daily and I felt like they thought they were a little more on the mighty side than those around them. Then I thought about them a little deeper, and started seeing patterns of severely unconfident and insecure behavior. Was it all a cover?

In a way, I instantly felt sorry for that person. Even if their attitude and approach with others frustrated me into fits, I could still see the pain that was cloaked in the shadows. I felt like the people who did not act as full of themselves ended up actually being happier at the end of the day, whether or not they boasted about it with a megaphone. Humility allows us to stop lying, and gives us the chance to be honest with ourselves. Finally, we get to be sincere with the rest of the world.

If this is the case all around us, then is it deranged to say that those people who act arrogant and mightier than others need reassurance that they are okay? Do they need told they are appreciated? It seems backward, and like we would only reinforce them, but who knows? One thing is for sure: I do not think that arrogant or excessively prideful behavior gets us far in our relationships with others. From being judgmental or bragging about oneself, to making fun of others, lack of humility has many masks. It performs year-round all over the world. Shall we stop giving it a standing ovation, and have it take a seat? I wish we would.

Count Your Blessings

I would like you to remember something for me. Think about the last time you were stressed. Many things can drag us through the mud over and under, from school and work to social drama and life's random accidents. There is a lot going on around us in our hellacious fish tank, and we often get very worn out from it. Think about the stress experienced from a situation where you have an essay due tomorrow, and a long night of work at your part-time job lies ahead of you before you will finally get to tackle that essay. Many of us would sigh, throw our hands up, and gripe. One person getting their ear full would not be enough, and the situation would probably climb to a rant you would carry on your tongue all day. This has the potential to be a frustrating day.

However, there was probably a teenage girl somewhere in the world that same day that was abducted from her natural life, addicted to some substance, raped repeatedly, and beaten. She will then later be sold into a life of sex slavery and will never again grasp another free breath or see her family again. Now, imagine how she feels about her day.

There was probably a boy overseas somewhere that same day that woke up that morning hungrier than he had ever been. He was so tired and dehydrated because he has not had regular access to clean drinking water for some time now. He may be five, six, seven years old and has no idea if his parents are alive or not because he has not seen them in years. And later that day he will die from starvation and disease, without a fighting chance in the world.

Are these examples a bit extreme? Maybe they are, but is it not the truth? From rape and murders to abduction and other life-crushing events, there is a lot that goes in this world that can make what we complain about seem so petty. In many cases, that is because we forget to step back and see the big picture. Yes I do it too. Actually, I find myself doing it a lot. This lack of appreciation is something I need to patch up. I need to keep everything positive on my mind and tongue, not my trivial problems and issues. However, we always find hang-ups and problems easier to hang onto, instead of spending time talking about everything that goes right each and every day.

When we remind ourselves to be more grateful we begin to become less greedy. As we learn to enjoy what we have, instead of becoming frustrated at what we haven't gotten yet, the world begins to brighten a little bit. With the right progression, this can make us a lot happier because we can become more internally satisfied. With less greed, more happiness, and a renewed sense of gratuity, what more could you ask for? I am sure those around you would not mind so much.

> "Blessed are those who give without remembering. And blessed are those who take without forgetting."
> —Bernard Meltzer

There are a lot of stories from my past I could reminisce about that remind me of this Pillar. One of these stories occurred during the summer of my internship at a Sherwin-Williams store in Tulsa. Throughout the previous school year at OSU I had grown to feel like I appreciated what I had. I felt that I was a fairly grateful person, until one of my co-workers put my life into a different perspective. Because this certain co-worker was affiliated with gang activity and does not want his name mentioned, we will just call him Darren.

I have never been the person from the richest of backgrounds, and sometimes I feel embarrassed of my origins compared to those around me at a state university. I had no idea Darren would snap my puny worries in half with the unhinging of his jaw. Gratuity tends to flow through people and their lives like a river, downstream and ever-moving.

I went into work that day in a flustered ball of woes about my financial situation. I did not have too much spending money, I had to work every day to cover all of my expenses over the summer, and my student loans were doing nothing but multiplying. I had also recently realized that I was not going to be able to do the summer trip with my friends that we had planned because I wasn't going to have enough excess cash. Then Darren came in to work.

I noticed right away that his face was swollen, and remembered that he had not been at work lately because he had surgery on his jaw. I found out that it had been broken in a fight with one of his best friends, and he had to go through a pretty extensive surgery to repair it. Darren could speak enough to be understandable, but his mouth had been wired shut to help with the healing process. This was the first bill he was going to have to pay. He also had to pay some sort of ticket issued by the police that was involved with the altercation. When I asked him what pain pills he was taking, he pulled out a bag of aspirin, and proceeded to tell me how he was going to have to crush these up and put them in some water. He could not even afford the pills that would keep him out of agonizing pain. He should not have been at work in his condition, but he had to be there. Darren had to be on the clock to make money and start the funding somewhere.

After I got him talking about his inability to buy medicine, I found out that he made less money than I did. This revelation floored me. I was just a summer intern between college semesters and was making better money than this guy. This man had a child, a girlfriend whom he lived with, the house that they shared, a car that they both had to share, and now all of these bills. Darren was barely making more than minimum wage.

Shortly after this situation, his water and power got shut off and he lost his cell phone service. He also got kicked out of his house for a short span of time. He had no money and was barely scraping by. I was griping because of my lack of extra spending money for the summer. I think I needed to learn how to count again; count my blessings, that is.

Yes, he was mad and upset about his situation. But I started looking at something that shook me to my core. He seemed to gripe about his money problem to others less than I complained about my situation to myself. I did not go around talking about my situation, but in a way, he was not as affected or dragged down by what he had to do. He was stronger in the face of such issues, and he probably appreciated each meal much more than I did. He probably valued the dollar bills in his back pocket far more gratefully than me. He had taught me such a lesson, and did not even know it. In a very real sense, I suddenly felt guilty. I felt so ungrateful.

"Men are slower to recognize blessings than evils."

—Titus Livy

At one point while at Oklahoma State University, there was a period of time where I was admittedly slightly depressed. I was very overwhelmed by the social and personal drama that swirled around me, the pressure from all of my classes, and my different involvements around campus. One of those major involvements was my Resident Assistant position and all of the extra things that it dashed onto my plate on a daily basis. I was so strung out, and I elaborate more on this situation in *Maintain Time for Yourself.*

What really helped me was realizing that I was being very ungrateful. I was here at a state university. I was lucky enough to be able to go to college in the United States. I had both legs, both arms, could talk well, had all of my senses, and I had both of my parents. This is just the beginning of the observations that I could mention. I had an infinite amount of things to be thankful for, but the handful of imperfections had so much accelerated gravity in them that they anchored me to the floor.

It all comes down to two things: perspective and appreciation. If we can step out of our shoes, walk over, and jump into someone else's shoes for a bit, then we can begin to see their world. Getting into the right frame of mind about how bad things truly could be is a valuable experience. We know the saying "It could be worse." If only we could be reminded every day just how true that statement really is.

I often wonder how people will sit in class and complain about the things that they do. I have heard people complaining about having to walk from certain classes or gripe about having to do homework. I have done this before, and realize just how ungrateful I sound when I hear hear other people doing the same thing. We are all at college, able to make it to these classes, and for the ultimate bottom line: we are all still alive. There are people who do not get to go to college, or who are not even fortunate enough to know what college is.

After we realize what others go through, we can then begin to appreciate our own lives. From the designer clothes on your back to the bottled water you can walk in anywhere and buy, we all have so much to appreciate. If you shrink your favorite shirt or jacket and get irate, think about those who have one shirt to their name. If you get stressed at work, remember that there are people who would kill to have your stress. There are those who would kill to have the stress of making a house payment. These are those who are homeless, and would fill your spot at your job in a heartbeat if given a chance. Admittedly, we all take advantage of what we have. I think it is natural for us to get accustomed to what we always see and play with. We get used to being spoiled; especially when it comes to money.

The way life seems to unravel around us usually leads to our gratuity coming from outside sources. Most of the time, appreciation will come after we interact with someone else or see things that end up reshaping our perceptions. We begin to twist things and rework how we feel about certain things we have or do. What if we were to make a push to have these kinds of things come from within, and not just be directed by the actions of others?

I was talking with one of my friends, Mike, about this past Christmas, and he said something that has stuck with me ever since. We often try to appreciate what we get for Christmas, or relish our Christmas day for what it is, even if it was not the best. This last

Christmas was surreal because it was my first one to celebrate with each of my parents separately, because of their recent split. This is what I had been telling people when we all exchanged stories about our Christmases. Then I asked Mike how his Christmas went.

His reply was one that left me staring at the floor. He told me how ecstatically happy he was this Christmas because it was the first time in eight to nine years that he was able to open actual wrapped presents on Christmas day. This did not even occur with his own family, because he and his mom had gotten into a fight on Christmas Eve and he had not spoken to her. It was actually made possible because he spent Christmas morning with his girlfriend's family. They bought him presents and wrapped them for him. He mentioned that it was all he could do not to cry from how happy it made him feel. He said to me, "Man, it was so cool. I had an actual, real Christmas. It was so nice."

I instantly thought about my last eight to nine Christmases: all of them included wrapped presents under a tree on that special morning. Gratuity burst in the room right when Mike said that, slapped me in the face, crossed its arms, and then glared at me for a bit while tapping its foot. The icing on the cold plate that I just got served was that Mike had to drop out of college just a month prior to this conversation because he could not even come close to affording it at the time, loans and all.

If we remember to be grateful, stop being greedy, count our blessings, and cherish every advantage we have, then we can begin to live a happier life. The less we worry with what we lack, and the more we focus on what we have, the more grateful we will naturally become. From minor possessions to the special people in your life, anything can be taken away. So please, cherish it. Cherish it all.

IT IS ALL ABOUT
HOW YOU REACT
TO THINGS

The world will throw everything
in its arsenal at you, and then some. How we react
to tragedies, our brightest moments, and everything
in between can be crucial.

CRITICISM COMES FROM SOLIDITY

"Unless you're getting criticized, you're not really doing much."

—Ophelia Jetta, woman entrepreneur
and guest speaker in my class
at OSU in Spring 2011

I have been criticized a lot in my life for many of the things that I have done or attempted to accomplish. It is a fact of life that if you stand up for yourself and say or do something, there will always be someone who does not like what you are doing, what you believe in, or what you want to accomplish. It is in these crucial moments of defiance and opposition that we, as people, have to stand for what we believe in and all the things we take to heart.

There are many things in my life I would defend to the bone for, especially many of the people around me. If we do not make a stand for what we believe in, then others will parade their views all over us. Courage and resolve both promote what it is that you truly stand for. It can be little things like the clothes we wear or even topics as encompassing as religion or politics. If we fall weak and waiver in our expressions and beliefs to please others, then we might as well not say anything.

A car, to some of us, is just what we use to get to and from places. To others it is an extension of who we are, and another outlet for us to be unique within ourselves. I have always taken a sense of pride in the fact that what I did to my cars was for internal reasons. Because I enjoyed doing it so much it was ever so worth it.

To illustrate this point, allow me to share with you the story of my first two vehicles.

If you are not a "car person" then much of this may seem a little silly to you. That is the ordeal though; people never see situations the same way. Put yourself in my shoes and relate it to some deep passion you may have. Photography, gardening, model-building, traveling, carpentry? We all have at least one.

I began loving cars at an early age, and by the time I got my hands on my first car I was foaming at the mouth to fix it up. My second (and current) car is something that I take a lot of personal joy and accomplishment from. I spent a lot of money and time making my car what it is today. Money is no longer dumped into it because I have been strapped for loose funds for some time now, as I am now becoming a senior in college at OSU. In addition to that, my second car has achieved a level of "completion" that I had desired from the beginning. I like how it looks now, and I think everything I did to it comes together nicely for a finished product. Again, that is simply my own opinion, and that is the picture that I paint.

My first car was a disaster. I tried dressing up and flashing out a 1993 Chevrolet Cavalier. It had custom blue tribal vinyl decals all over the hood and down the sides of the car, Wal-Mart hubcap "rims," and a few other cheap add-ons. The icing on the cake for the entire mantra of my first car was how it got its infamous name, "The Ghini". I put Lamborghini decals and logos on my car in all the corresponding places where the Chevrolet emblems had previously been to make them seem legitimate; sarcasm at its finest. Everyone else laughed and enjoyed the mockery when they saw the emblems said Lamborghini and realized what they were witnessing.

As time went on and people poked fun at me more and more, the humor of the Lamborghini joke somehow started to fade. I got made fun of at school, in parking lots, and even as I was driving down the street. If the decals did not get noticed, the white car decorated with bright blue decals did. People either loved it or they absolutely hated it.

Laughing it off and thinking that people were enjoying the joke alongside me only lasted so long. Unfortunately for me and my humor-driven investment, that was not the case. People were laughing at me for what I had tried to do and not just because of the intended joke. They mocked my car and thought I was trying to play the whole thing off as if it may be real, or as if I thought my car was true Lamborghini material. Fire spreads fast and kids are fast to point out flaws or inconsistencies in others.

The police officer who pulled me over and gave me my first moving violation was sure to make fun of the Lamborghini stickers as well. She kept remarking about how fast my car must be and how many women I must get with my expensive and exotic car. Now even police officers were joining in the mockery. There was no way I was going to be able to clean this entire mess up one person at a time. What was I going to do? I could not pull each and every single person over and give them a brief disclaimer and explanation of my car and its inside joke. The leaning tower of pressure began to fall, and my house of cards crumbled with the slightest of breezes.

In my fit of weakness I took off the Lamborghini emblems and logos from the grill, rear windshield, back part of the trunk, and sides of the car. I did not want my car to be a joke anymore. As far as I was concerned, this car was now to be taken seriously from this point on for how it looked, and for its uniqueness. When all of my friends found out what I had done, they were disappointed. They had loved the joke and enjoyed it. For me, the joke had run its course and I wanted people to actually like my car for what I had done to it. Little did I know at the time, that I missed the true reason the entire time.

Not much changed. The mockery switched from the Lamborghini remarks to comments about my crappy Cavalier that supposedly attempted to be some wannabe *Fast and the Furious* knock-off. People did not understand why I would ever want to put blue stickers all over my car. I had attempted to switch the stance and reputation of my car but nothing improved. My original joy was destroyed and I ruined what I had originally built for myself to try and please others.

I was young and cared so much about what other people thought and said about me and my car. Any person who has put money into their car knows the feeling of wanting people to like it. It is the same feeling we would get when people would give us compliments after obtaining a new haircut or new outfit. We just want the changes to not only be accepted, but appreciated.

At this point I was just at a loss and accepted my fate at face value. I just enjoyed my car for what it was, and accepted the occasional sincere compliment from someone who liked what I had done. I never had sight of what I should have done about the jesting, but in hindsight it is all 20/20. I should have just enjoyed what I stood for and let the Lamborghini emblems fly. My car broke down once and for all, about a year after I got it. "The Ghini" or not, the issue was dead in the water.

I knew I couldn't go without a car for long and immediately started looking for "The Ghini's" replacement. My second car was going to be paid for by myself, and I was going to get it financed. I also knew that what I was going to get was not going to be another *Ghini* situation like the one I had just endured. It is funny how things seem to turn out sometimes, is it not?

> "A man who stands for nothing will fall for anything."
> —Malcolm X

It took me all of three hours to pick out my second car. It was during the summer before my senior year of high school, which would have been the summer of 2007. My second car was also a Cavalier, but this one was a 2002 Ecotec LS. In other words, I thought it was a lot nicer. It had a sunroof, power everything, a CD player, and other nice features my first car did not seem to have. I was so happy, and even liked the really obnoxious yellow color that it sported. My vision was instantly starting to launch, and within two months of having the car I got a new paint job, along with an entire overhaul of the car itself.

The look of my car completely changed all at once. I turned it over to a shop in Tulsa with all the parts and modifications I had prepared. It was a whole new machine when I picked it back up. There were all sorts of body modifications put on the car, from a body kit to a new spoiler on the trunk, as well as a brand new paint job inspired by a 1995 Jeep color by the name of Bright Mango. Over the next two years, I added on several other things (including a black paint job elaborated on in *Harbor Love Not Hate*) to finish out the vision for my car, which ended up being coined "The Dark Cavy."

With the aggressive changes, bright colors, neon lighting, and unique sound of my exhaust this car received plenty of attention from the time it pulled out of the shop, like my first car. Negative attention came once again, as expected. Everything got made fun of from the neon lighting to the large wing-shaped spoiler on the trunk. The orange pinkish color it had for a while, before going black, was not spared from ridicule either. However, I did not waiver this time and stood by my decisions. I defended myself when necessary and knew why I did each and every thing that I had done. I had not customized my car for them; I had done it for me.

My car was not just something I thought about when I needed to get to work or school and back. It was a passion of mine and something I cared for. We all have things we care about that help make us unique, and I was no different. So, what is it for you?

In Owasso and the surrounding areas, there were two groups of people in the car scene that seemed to dominate the majorities. There were the imports and the muscle cars. The imports consisted of cars that were often very low to the ground had suspension work, maybe an extension on the front bumper to slightly lower it, and different wheels. The other side of the fence included the muscle car category populated with powerful and loud cars that were made here in America. The dilemma for the car I created was that it was in the middle of the two groups I just mentioned. Neither side liked what I had done with my car, and it seemed like acceptance was sometimes a mere fantasy.

Needless to say, I got mocked and disapproved by both sides of the fence. My car was in the middle of the two current norms. People made fun of me for trying to make a Cavalier look fast or powerful and I was told that my spoiler was bigger than my car. People told me that I spent way too much money on a car that was as "low quality" as mine. I heard that my car was crappy "just because." They did not need a specific reason to attack me or the things that I cared about, and sometimes it was just for spite.

This is something that means a lot to me, so I was going to care what others said about it and I let it get under my skin sometimes; a lot of the time. That is exactly what they wanted, and they often succeeded.

Here is where I make my case. In the light of all the opposition and jokes I received from having my car the way it is, I attempted to not change or falter in the face of adversity. I tried to not change myself this time around, and I simply rolled with what I was dealt and made the best of it. I tried to see where people may be coming from or why they might say certain things, but I never changed my car based on their opinions. For that, I have made enemies.

As ridiculous as it may sound to some, I have people back in Owasso who hate me because of my car. Today I still get revved at by other cars, stared or pointed at, mocked, or teased for certain things about my car that others may find a problem with.

I have always tried to be very respectful about others' cars because of what I have experienced with my vehicles along the way. I will usually not bring the negatives of someone else's car up, and instead focus on what I do like, and compliment that. It is respectful to act in such a manner, and I know how it felt when someone else did not have that same humility and respect for me.

There is another group of people who disagree with this kind of story. Many individuals think doing anything as extensively aftermarket (such as vehicle customization) as I did to a car is wrong, a waste of money, and/or useless. These specific people feel like a vehicle is for getting from point A to point B, and that is all.

My rebuttal to such a statement is that the car I drive every day just happens to be a passion and hobby of mine. Because of this, I take a certain joy from how I have customized my car and how I now get to experience it every time I walk outside. I love to have a car that looks like it does because of what I have dreamed and crafted. It is one of my very own ways that I get to be an artist.

Think about this. What in your life do you care a lot about, that some or maybe even all of those people around you do not seem to understand? What do the people around you care more about than you do? What are their passions, creations, aspirations, and hobbies that they believe in? I do not think my car is amazing or world-changing, but I do think that it being customized the way I wanted allows it to stand out and mean so much to me. It is, in a very distinct way, my very own creation.

Customizing my vehicle means a lot to me because it becomes so personal to me. I love being creative and expressing my creativity in a multitude of different ways; customizing the vehicle I drive every day is just one more way I am able to do that. When I see the project finished that I spent a lot of time and effort bringing together, it brings me a good sense of achievement and completion. People obtain this satisfaction or express their creativity in a plethora of different ways. Music, art, gardening, housework, writing, making films, sewing, scrap-booking, building new items, fixing broken things, or even sports are just a few examples of hobbies or things people around us do that they very well may take pride in. What do you do that you take personally?

> "Don't back down just to keep the peace. Standing up
> for your beliefs builds self-confidence and self-esteem."
> —Oprah Winfrey

People can question or attempt to tear down what I have established. At the end of the day, they can never take away what I stand for, no matter what it may be. It could be about my friends, my religious beliefs, the way I dress, where I was raised, or anything. My resolve and care reside within me, and through solidity comes a stance and a cause. Our solidity is a cause worth standing up for. If people can relate their own passions and what they stand for with ours, then they can begin to understand them. This is what we must all struggle to do for others, even when we oppose their opinions.

We would desire the same respect and humility from them. Relating is understanding.

What would you stand up for in a room full of people who remained seated? What would you do if people stood up just to speak against you even standing up in the first place? For example, think about three things in your life you truly believe in and would defend whole-heartedly. These passions and things we truly take to heart give us great joy, and we must hold on to them with solidity. When you stand up for yourself people will notice, and many will stand up too. They will not always be with you, and a lot of the time if they are not with you, they will try to get you to sit back down. Please stay standing, and do it for both of us.

HOLD RESPECT FOR OTHERS

We have always heard to "respect your elders." But I say, *why not respect everyone?* Why do parents not tell their kids that? I understand that the common saying simply emphasizes helping and being generous to older individuals because they are more experienced and are supposed to be wiser than we are. However, respect is a broad term and can apply to many aspects of our lives, both grand and miniscule. We can give others respect simply by not being rude, by displaying selfless behavior, or by refraining from talking negatively about someone when they are not around.

Perhaps honoring people also relates to doing something for others, not because they asked you to or because you wanted to perform a favor for them, but because you know it would be what they would *want* you to do. Often times, being respectful is something that goes completely unnoticed. In a way, respect can be refraining from doing something.

If we refrain for someone else it is for reasons involving them and who they are. Our behavior becomes completely about others. It would be respectful to refrain from yelling out random statements at a funeral. It would be considered respectful to refrain from talking during or disturbing the national anthem. If we wanted to act out differently, but did not, those desires would stay a secret. Keeping it that way would, in turn, be respectful.

> "I'm not concerned with your liking or disliking me. All
> I ask is that you respect me as a human being."
> —Jackie Robinson

We should strive to keep that mentality with us at all at times during our various situations we face day in and day out. We would all like to be respected at our jobs, in our classes, and in our own homes. So shall we return the favor, or just expect it from others? It is hard to respect a disrespectful person, plain and simple. I have struggled with respect as a maturing teenager, but I recently received a very worthy test for my values on the issue. It has to deal with my father and our relationship as I grew up with him.

When I was a little guy I wanted to grow tall and be big and strong like my dad. I wore little matching cowboy shirts and cowboy hats like him, picked up his sayings, and challenged him in arm wrestling matches every night. He was courteous and allowed me to win sometimes. He wore cowboy boots and I had little pairs of my own. He had a recliner in front of the TV. I had a miniature one. I emulated him, and was proud of it.

Somewhere between six and ten years of age, with the social pressures of school and my own style preferences, I stopped wearing any of that stuff. I cared about things differently than he did, valued different traditions, and we started to not see eye-to-eye on a lot of things. As I advanced through my teen years we started growing distant for many reasons and I began to not respect my father. I frequently talked back to him, and when he overreacted about something, I was sure to let him know I thought so in a sarcastic tone. It wasn't the type of behavior that could go ignored for long.

As time went on, I became annoyed with his views on life, which were very different than mine. As a young teenager, I liked to spend my paychecks on things like my car and hanging out with friends. He said I should be saving all of my money. I spent money on a lot of things, and most of it was stuff he did not approve of, such as my video camera for filming, my new TV, video games, and new clothes every fall for school. By my junior year of high school our relationship was anything but prospering.

I did not respect his wishes and did what I wanted to do because I thought it was right. I would get annoyed with him when he would attempt to lecture me on all the ways I was messing up. I often felt like he did not care about the intricacies of my evolving adolescent life. His lack of patience and understanding infuriated me, and it had gotten to a point where I just lost respect for the man.

My parents were talking about divorce for reasons I will leave unsaid. My mom wanted to file and my dad was pleading her to reconsider. I wanted my mom to leave my father because I had grown spiteful towards him. I ignored him, made snide remarks, and I liked to treat him negatively when he would scold me for something. I did not want my mom to have to live with the man I had grown to distrust and dislike. I did not want to have to live in the same small house of one thousand square feet with an increasingly unhappy marriage and a man I could not respect or even enjoy to be around.

This man was my own father, and I still had felt this way. It is my worst fear, as a future father, that my child will treat me like I did my own father back then; that very idea was perhaps what awakened me to reality.

Through various situations over my senior year of high school and the following summer, something started happening as my parents decided to work things out and avoid divorce. My perceptions were being sculpted and transformed as my mentality started to switch from a high-school teen to that of an eager college student. I began seeing things my father did differently, and some of the things he resembled began to appear differently to me. He was not acting any different; I was just changing my mind about the way I should treat him.

I started to realize I was just being a punk when I had lashed out at him. Previously, I had just been acting out as a typical, rebellious, "always right" teenager who saw his dad as a joke. But I had seen much more in life and realized how well of a job he did raising, caring for, and fostering me compared to some fathers out there. Those surreal experiences at the end of high school, such as graduation, reminded me that he will be gone someday. I will miss his jokes, mannerisms, and all of our shared stories. I did not want the time to come for my dad to be gone and I not have found my respect for him.

Throughout this transitional period I started to understand his frugal ways were largely because of his childhood. He grew up in a very poor environment for the entire first period of his life. My dad struggled with finances and he worked very hard for every dollar he earned in life before he retired. He had to save for emergencies and harder times than I ever had to experience. He did not have the financial ease I did when I was seventeen years old. I also tried to be patient with his quick temperament and his ability to be so apathetic with everything in my life. We dressed and talked differently, had different ethics and perspectives, and we were totally different men. That was our difference.

I may have not worn cowboy boots anymore, drove a truck, or wore flannel shirts and Wrangler jeans, but I had started to see why he valued those things. He ended up having a three-hundred-and-twenty square foot exterior room in the backyard built for me to live in. It included a bathroom, so I could practically just live out in my own external room. I could stay there while going to Rogers State, and give my parents (and myself) more privacy.

This helped my parents out by giving them more space and privacy and my dad saw the ways his frugal mindset had constricted his own marriage. He still did not get very involved with any aspect of my life, but I tried to understand his style of parenting, as well as his own unique personality. I could try to respect our differences and leave it at that. He wasn't a whole new man, by any means, but I was; I was a new man who had found that respect for my dad.

My dad raised me and provided a lot for me. He could have helped my mother or his other kids from his first marriage much more than he did over the years, but he did more than some fathers. It caused a lot of stress on my mother and me, as well as his other kids, but that is something we will all have to live with. My dad and I are not close by any means, but I do not have disdain for him or his ways. I respect his past and his decisions, even if I do not agree with them.

We are distantly spread on two completely different social, cultural, financial, generational, and emotional levels. I have come to appreciate that. There was a new bond of respect forming that had not previously been there, but its strength was about to be tested in a very sudden and unexpected sort of way.

"This is the final test of a gentleman: his respect for those who can be of no possible service to him"
—William Lyon Phelps

It was the first week of August 2010. It was about ten days before I transferred colleges and moved from home to go to OSU. I had recently been interested in becoming closer with my half-brother, David, after having conversations with my mom during the drive back from seeing family one weekend. During this talk, I had also learned a lot of dark things about past events in my mother's side of the family. It was a weird transitional time period of swirling thoughts and wonders.

David was one of five children my father had from his first marriage, and growing up I had seen him once a year every Christmas. I had never seen my half-siblings too often while growing up, and I was not necessarily ever that close to any of them.

I was at a point in my life where I wanted to be closer to that side of my family; I never really knew them, and I regretted that. I told my mom that to get in better contact with my siblings I could start by having lunch with David. He was always the sibling I related to the most when I saw everyone, and it was always easier for me to talk with him. David was my brother, and I felt like I did not know him at all. I got his phone number from my mom and promptly called him.

The night before I was supposed to meet David for lunch, my mom texted me and said she wanted to tell me something. She wanted me to drop by her office at work the next morning before going to lunch. She stated that she had something to tell me and that she wanted to do so in person. I was nervous and a little confused by all this, but I went along with it. The next morning I drove to my mom's work, went to her office, and she had me sit down as she closed the door to her office. I felt like a child again, being sat down in the principal's office.

My mom looked shaken with slight fear and nervousness. She was smiling a lot to cover these uneasy feelings, and it scared me too. My mom and I have always shared contagious emotions, so it shook me up a little. I had no idea what she was about to share with me. She began talking about how I wanted to have lunch with David because he was my brother and family by blood. I thought maybe she was about to tell me something bad about David, or maybe she would be warning me about wanting to become closer with him or something. I was way off.

Instead my mom revealed to me something she had waited years to say; twenty to be exact. She told me that my dad, the man I grew up with, was not my biological father.

I had no idea what to say. I just sat there, in wonder. It all started to make some sort of surreal sense though. I was built differently than both of my parents, but the thought of something like this had never crossed my mind. There had really not ever been any reason for it to have crossed my mind, though. My mom proceeded to tell me that my biological father was a man who donated to a sperm bank years ago, and that she was a recipient. We have one certificate with a few facts about him, not including his name or identity, and that is all I will ever know.

The dad I had grown up with had been "fixed" before he married my mom, and my mom wanted a child; that child was me. That was how I was born, and I learned this as my life was already ever-changing at the age of twenty. I cried the whole time I was driving to lunch because of the overwhelming amount of emotion that overcame me. It did not hurt me; it was just such an odd experience, and one that bewildered me. I felt like I was in a crucial scene in a movie, or like MTV was doing a one hour special on my life. But I was just experiencing the same thing many other children and young adults have experienced, or will experience some day. If you can relate I know how you felt. I believe that I handled it well, however, and understood why this had all happened and why I was told when I was.

You may be asking yourself how this integrates with respecting my father. Well the hardest part on my mom in this whole situation was already over; telling me. The hardest part for my dad was not over yet. He did not know I knew all of this at this point. The question now was: how and when do I reveal to him that I now know the truth?

My mom had explained to me that my dad was so nervous about this, and had delayed telling me for years and years. My dad was always someone who did not think about things that he did not want to; he would shove negative issues under a rug. This was yet another thing I did not agree with, but I digress. He had denied telling me for years, but my mom thought it was time. She wanted to do it at this time because of my pursuits involving David, and the fact that I would be leaving home less than two weeks later for OSU. She told my dad that I needed to be told sometime soon, but she never told him she had decided to tell me on that day.

My dad did not want me to know for several reasons, one being our past. He feared resentment from me if I found out that he was not my biological father. He thought I would resist him and that our relationship may recede to what it had been when I was a rebellious young adolescent, or maybe even worse. He did not want to risk me having bad feelings towards him, or me exiling him from my life. So, out of respect for his worries and concerns, I had an idea.

If my dad's fear about letting me know was that I would resent him afterwards, then I was not going to tell him that I knew, at least not right away. I thought I could wait and let him know at a different time; maybe a year or so down the road? I wanted to show my dad that on the day I told him, I would have already known for quite some time, and he would see that it did not change the way I treated him at all.

Do not get me wrong; it is quite surreal looking at him and talking with him now and thinking about the fact that I will never truly know my biological father. But I do not resent him for that, and I do not feel any differently towards him. He is still my dad.

And yes, I still call him dad. Even in my head and to my mom, he is still known as dad. He was there for my birth, helped raise me, and even changed my diapers. He has played an active role throughout my life and he has supported me through various times.

He is the husband of my mother, and he raised me and treated me like I was his own.

I will not treat him differently, or hold him in any different light. He may not be my biological father, but he is my dad. He was always my father that was there for my first haircut, my first day of school, and for my graduation. He always has been, and always will be, my dad.

As I write this now, he still does not know that I know the truth. However, by the time I *finish* this book, he will. I will tell him that it has been around a year since I was told the truth, and he will know it did not affect the way I treat him. He will be at rest about it, and he will not worry about the day any longer that I am told about my origins. I've known for a while now, dad, and I love you.

> "People are respectable only as they respect."
> —Ralph Waldo Emerson

If I were a father in the position of my own, I would have loved if someone had that thought for me, and that is what this is all about. When is the last time you felt respected? Or what is something you feel like you should be honored for, at least a little bit? We all have something.

Is there anything in your life at this moment that you could start doing to hold more respect in your life? If we all make a conscious effort to hold respect in our daily lives, I think we would start seeing the rewards instantly. This has been an issue I have wrestled with throughout my life, from adolescence to what is now supposed to be adulthood. I love it when I feel respected, and it is a good feeling. I am sure you feel the same way. So shall we all strive to return the favor?

Respect stems from acting for others, and in a way, being selfless. If we can refrain from acting in a way we would like to, or a way that is natural, for someone else then we are being respectful. It does not trample on liberties or rights because it is our choice to hold respect. The more respect we hold and show the more we are likely to receive. It's a fair trade.

HARBOR LOVE, NOT HATE

Growing up, you may have heard that hate and love are not that different. People told us they are not too far from each other. In contrast with that statement, I would say they take completely different tolls on our hearts, moods, and our blood pressures.

This is a theme and chapter I can say that I still struggle with to this day. I sometimes find it hard to let go of those memories that incite instant frustration and defensive feelings. It is challenging to just forgive and forget when someone took advantage of me, tarnished my respect, or trampled all over me. There is one elusive and sometimes difficult thing that seems to be the tipping point in this situation: forgiveness.

Forgiveness can help us let go of a grudge, set things aside, and stop brewing over past events that weigh us down. The question I always ask at this point, when someone tells me to forgive someone, is, "What if they did something I do not want to forgive them for? What if they do not deserve any forgiveness?" We all have struggles with this question and probably always will. Who have you not forgiven yet?

> "Forgiveness is an attribute of the strong."
> —Mohandas Gandhi

There seems to be no secret to handling this issue; none at all. Negative feelings will come at us in every different form, shape, and disguise. Disdain will lead us down all sorts of paths, all of them negative. We just have to keep certain things in mind, like this:

we have to know that a year down the road it will be a completely different time and situation, and we will see everything as an entirely different world. So when it comes to letting go of hatred against others, the sooner the better. Easier said than done, I know. I know all too well.

Harboring hate just inflicts pain upon ourselves and demeans others. Imagine our spirit as a balloon and our harbored hatred as a lead weight. Expending so much energy on hate weighs us down, plain and simple. Consider this: if you hated someone because of something they did to you, they will probably just live their life in peace. Most of the time, they will not be worrying about what they did to you. And you, the supposed victim of the situation, will be the one constantly afflicted and plagued by that darkened heart of yours. It does not make sense for us to hurt ourselves like that. They do not magically feel our hate from miles away, and they are not telepathically afflicted. It is useless and negative for us to stew like that in spite of them. So let us try to hinder that mindset and attitude, as well as those feelings.

There have been many situations in my life that have caused frustration toward others. There have been several instances throughout my time growing up where I was caused great grief, pain, or hurt by the actions and words of others. The stories I will share with you are just two of these instances and examples I hope you will be able to relate with. Before I even start, think to yourself: who is someone that you dislike? Do they know how you feel? You know who they are.

Now take a moment to ponder about the difference in two social situations. When you talk about someone you do not like and possibly even hate, what kind of mood do you find yourself in? Do you get annoyed just talking or even thinking about them? What sort of tone and inflection is noticeable in your voice? Contrast those observations with the times when you talk about someone you adore and truly like. In those times, you become happy and probably smile a lot. There is a big difference in your underlying mood here.

There are two people who lived in Owasso who I came to despise over time. These two people and the reasons I came to hate each of them have nothing to do with one another. Some will disagree with my actions in these two stories. Some people will laugh at some of the things that happened, or something that was said. To be honest, I still laugh a little about some of it. I may struggle from time to time with situations like these, but I am trying. My heart is in it, which I think is the most crucial part.

The first story is one that involves a lot of external implications and consequences. Of my past, it is one of my most frequently told stories, because my friends always bring it up to others or people will ask how and why I got my car painted black from orange. The person I will be discussing is someone I have had a lot of time to try to forgive and he is someone I knew from high school. The initial event took place during my senior year of high school. He was a grade younger than me, and I did not know him at all-until one night. His name is Justin.

I used to take part in the elusive and trivial activity of yelling at people from a moving car. We did this for our own childish enjoyment and to get ridiculous or humorous reactions from our "victims." In those days, it was one of our favorite past times and was a solid foundation for many of our funniest memories as a group of friends. We have probably yelled anything you could ever think of at least once over the years. In Owasso, there were always groups of guys who would gather in parking lots, stand around their cars, and just hang out together. I happened to know that a lot of the guys I did not like from school were sometimes involved in these big hangouts.

Needless to say, these groups became targets for our yelling shenanigans while we circled them like vultures. Often, some of the people in these big, parking-lot-loitering parties would chase us, or yell something back. Sometimes they even threw things at us, but it was never anything more than we thought we could handle. Until one night, that is.

One night at a *Kum and Go* gas station in Owasso, there was a group of about twenty kids hanging out in the parking lot. I saw that a lot of the cars there in the crowd belonged to people I did not like. These kids were members of the "car scene" and were some of those who made my life as a custom-Cavalier-driver hellacious. We pulled up to the group, and as my car stopped, they all looked up. This felt like a movie moment in the making.

> "Hanging onto resentment is letting someone you despise live rent-free in your head."
>
> —Ann Landers

Before I go any further, let me just clarify that not all of our yelling situations were hateful. Indeed, many and maybe even most of the things we yelled were light-hearted and in a joking manner. We would sometimes just yell random gibberish, high five people from a moving car, or give loud and boisterous compliments to pedestrians while passing them on the road. However, this time was different. There were people there who teased me for my car. I was spiteful and had a point to make, even if I knew it was not right to do so.

As my car rolled to a stop, they all looked up, and I paused. I felt how nervous I was. "I didn't know the 'Piece of Shit Car Club' met here," I said. In the half second of reaction I watched, they all just stared. I then threw out a one-burst, gusty sarcastic laugh, as if I had just severely scoffed at them. I looked forward and drove off like a mad scientist blasting off into the future. As I flew out from the parking lot, my friend and front passenger, Kody, sat up. He and Jeremy, my friend in the back seat, and I shared a good laugh. No one was chasing us. Mission accomplished.

Jeremy wanted some Taco Bueno, which was right down the street, so we drove there immediately after our little stunt. He was inside getting his food because the drive-thru was backed up. As Kody and I waited in the parking lot, some guy was standing behind my car, taking pictures of it, and was on the phone laughing. I had no idea what he was doing but I tried to ignore him. Bad idea.

A minute later, two cars pulled up on both sides of us. These kids stared at me and were also laughing. I thought for a second, and then I realized something. It was them-the kids I had just yelled at. And there were three cars full of them. It was time to leave, whether or not Jeremy was still inside getting his food. I threw the car in reverse and sped out of the parking lot, going around the third car of angry teenagers.

It was at this point, while speeding down the main streets of Owasso, I realized I may have yelled at the wrong people this time. At two separate red lights, with my doors locked, some of the kids in pursuit ran up to my car, banged on the windows, and told me to get out. *Right, let me get right on that.* I continued driving and thought maybe they would stop chasing us after a half mile or so like everyone else usually did. Not this time.

I decided at this moment that taking a general route towards the Owasso police station would probably be a good idea. It couldn't hurt, at least. As I headed down the last street towards the station, a four lane road, they pulled a pretty good move. They boxed me in on three sides with their vehicles, one of them being a Camaro SS, and tried to force me to a stop. I decided to take a risk and dart left into a large neighborhood I had never quite navigated through.

I had no idea what I was doing or where I was going. What I did know was that I was going much faster than the neighborhood's twenty-five miles per hour speed limit and I was panicking. As we all blew stop signs and sped through the neighborhood at dangerous speeds, they managed to get in front of me once again with the Camaro, and I had to make another rash decision and turn left again. A cul-de-sac.

The chase was over, and now I was nothing but a trapped animal. I went down to the end of the cul-de-sac, turned around and drove back a little bit. I stopped the car, put it in park, double checked the fact that the doors were locked, and watched four guys slink over to my vehicle. Three cars were blockading the exit of the cul-de-sac, and I was not going to try anything now. Call me a coward, but I was not going to step out of the car and face several guys who just reenacted an episode of *COPS* to catch me. They were obviously pissed and now they wanted to do something about it. I am all for my honor and such, but I did not have any health insurance. No, thank you.

They began yelling profanities and insults, banged and shook my car, and told me to step out at least twenty different times. They were persistent. I was in a weakened and obviously scared state by this point, so I just sat there. Kody, still in the passenger's seat, was also visibly shaken and had no better idea of what to do than I did.

I rolled down the window an inch or two in an attempt to reason with them a bit and say something. My first personal interaction with the guy this whole story is about, Justin, was right at this moment. As I started to speak up, he spat in my face. At that moment I pulled out my phone and called the police. Even from outside the car, my harassers could see that I had dialed 911, and they began taking off. They wanted nothing to do with the police.

As they took off, they threw a few drinks at my car, sharing a cackle. I just sat there, frozen. Kody and I just looked at each other and knew that what we just experienced would become a story we would share forever. Nothing this serious had happened before in our history of drive-by yelling. It was a surreal and sort of humorous feeling. And besides, Jeremy was still at Taco Bueno, with no idea of why we left him or where we went. We could not help but laugh about that.

Shortly thereafter, the police arrived. They asked me if I wanted to press charges, but I denied the chance. There was no point. One of them insisted I check over the car with a flashlight, seeing as how it was eleven o'clock at night by now. There was a big crack on my driver's side door, and the paint was pretty messed up in the surrounding areas. In the process of trying to get me out, one of the assailants body slammed my door, cracking the paint on my door. After seeing that, I wanted to press some charges.

Kody and I rode with one of the officers, and I watched as Justin was arrested. I saw several others get arrested as well, and they were all brought to city hall for questioning and processing. I ended up pressing charges, filing a police report, and putting out the minor lawsuit for fixing my car at $990, the price to fix the damages done. I knew this whole situation was not over, and I would be seeing more of Justin. He and I had not even had a chance to get acquainted yet.

The funny thing about the situation is that all three of the guys I pressed charges against were strangers to me before that night. They just happened to be in the crowd of people I yelled at, and they were upset about what I said to them. At this point, you can argue about who deserved what that night, but that is not the point of this story. We rarely plan out things like this; the events that bring us harm, hurt, frustration, or bewilderment. It is not merely the event we must contemplate, but our reaction as well.

I used the money to get the new paint job, but there was some technicality to this situation. Due to error by the officer who happened to be working on my case, I only got settlement money from two of the guilty individuals. He forgot to send out the prosecution statement for the third individual due to some name mix-ups. This means I only ended up getting two-thirds of my settlement amount, and one of those who paid happened to be Justin. After talking with the paint shop and taking a risk, I decided not to fix the internal door damage and just to use the money to repaint my car black. I had been considering a new paint job for my car for a while, and what better an opportunity?

The next day at school, after the night the events in question had taken place and long before the money was processed over, Justin was looking for me. He had a sort of vendetta, I guess you could say. Justin found me in the hall and walked right up to me, cussing me out and trying to intimidate me. For some reason, it did not rattle my cage too much. I enjoyed showing him a smile and making him even angrier than he already was. Justin was controlled by his rage, and I was just fine knowing I was going to have my car fixed, with his money. He was sure to let me know I would not be smiling for long.

> "Hate is too great a burden to bear. It injures the hater more than it injures the hated."
>
> —Coretta Scott King

As the days passed by, the harassment did not ease up. He was getting his friends to harass me and try to intimidate me now. Unlike Justin, these guys were taller than me. He kept telling me to drop the charges and would glare at me as I walked past him in the halls. I remember once responding, "No man, you got to buy me a new paint job, remember? I'm sure you do." I laughed and just walked away once again. I used a smug demeanor to purposely upset him and make him hate me even more. It was my own fault. I also remember one of his huge friends, who was on the football team, walking up and telling me that he thought I deserved what I got that night. This kid was known for causing fights in school, and he was also known for always winning those fights. I tried to think quickly, fearing for my face, and responded, "Hit me, and I'll sue you too. Then you two could pay me at the same time?"

I hated this attention and constant fear of having to deal with one of these guys trying to get me to repeal my charges, so I told the school principle about the entire situation and he agreed that things were getting out of hand. He talked to Justin and threatened suspension if anything like this continued happening anymore on the school grounds. After this, he stared at me in the halls and parking lot, flipped me off, or pointed and called me names. This is when my true hatred toward him began. His attitude turned from hatred about the charges to making a mockery of me and my situation. He was teasing me, even though he knew I got what I wanted. To himself, Justin was still winning. It was working, though. I was getting fed up with him.

It was from this point on that I tried to one-up him all the time. I would say some smart-ass comment to him or flash another smile his way just to irk him a bit. On the sunny afternoon I got my car back, sporting its new shiny black coat, guess who I happened to run into? I saw him in the Arby's drive-thru as I pulled out of the parking lot of my local bank in Owasso. I drove right up next to his truck as he sat in the drive-thru line. My window was down, my shades were on, and I felt pretty good. He usually traveled in a group, but this time he was by himself and vulnerable. I piped up, "Hey man! Thanks again for the paint job. Looks great!" As I drove away, he flipped me off (his specialty), and if looks could kill, I would have been shot dead that day. I had temporarily won and felt good about it. I had just put down someone that I did not like.

Even though these moments may feel victorious for a second or two, we must realize that this euphoric sense of winning is merely temporary. These events rob the true enjoyment from our lives, and ultimately our hearts. This type of enjoyment we feel shows something slightly scary and intimidating: we begin to enjoy being hateful. We begin to like putting others down, and the mentality and psyche of it all takes over regardless of whether we dislike that person or not. It can be a dangerous and misleading road.

For the next two years, Justin and I had many encounters. They would always be completely random situations, but it would always be somewhere in Owasso. He would always yell at me, flip me off (he was becoming a real pro), or make fun of me and my car with anywhere from two to six people backing him up, just laughing. However, he never did anything to me physically; he was all talk. He made fun of me, my friends, and called me countless names. Resentment against him grew each time I came into contact with him. I found him arrogant and such a plague to my good moods every time he showed his face around me. In retrospect, I had only done this all to myself. I hated him for it, though. That was the easy thing to do.

I was just spiteful at this point. I did not regret getting my car painted one bit, because I did not feel like the verbal assault I had given that first night was grounds for him and his friends to make a piñata out of my vehicle. But, as time went on, something changed.

As college drew near, I found myself maturing. My grasp on many realities of the world was tightening, and I had come to realize that I was such a punk for everything that I had done as a teenager. I did feel bad for initiating the situation, and I learned to forgive him. Time healed the wounds left over from my interactions with him, and I thought about how I had never thought about what it may be like to be him. I did not know his home life. I did not know anything about his past, his desires, or anything. We were strangers.

It got to a point where I just wanted his acceptance for some odd reason and I wanted him to forgive me. I was at OSU in Stillwater at this point, and he was still in Owasso. How does anyone look someone else up these days? Facebook. I reluctantly sent him a friend request and waited. When he accepted my request, he sent me a short message full of bad grammar, sinister language, and hateful threats. He told me I was lucky he did not come and find me. I was a little offended and put off, and I contemplated how to reply to him.

My reply touched on several things, including how I had dropped all the hard feelings toward him and about the various situations we had shared. I elaborated on how I had changed my opinions over time, and how I had made an effort to drop my resentment for him. I mentioned how I requested him on Facebook because I wanted no problems between us anymore and mentioned our run-in at QuickTrip.

I had encountered him a few months before our messages at a QuickTrip. He just looked at me when he saw me. I thought maybe he did not recognize me, but he must have. It puzzled me, and I had no idea why he would react the way he did over Facebook after seeing me a few months prior. There was never any response to my rebuttal on Facebook, and I wondered for months what it would be like the next time we ran into each other.

A friend's step-father passed away recently. While leaving the funeral, I noticed that Justin was also there. We made eye contact, and given the current situation, he was the last thing on my mind. He looked at me blankly, then turned and mingled with his friends. Two weeks later, after moving back home from OSU for the summer, I drove past him in Owasso. He waved. The funny, and maybe cheesy thing was, that he waved a peace sign at me. I chuckled and finally felt at ease about it all.

We are on decent terms now, I suppose. It is refreshing to not have one more enemy out there. What I did back then was childish. Even though I have grown up a lot since then, I still have a lot more growing up and learning to do. I know that, for me, it has released some tension and aggravation when I think about him or the aforementioned situations. I feel like I could respect him if I talked to him now, and I think he sees it too. I asked him over Facebook if I could use his name in this book, and he said yes. So in case Justin ever reads this book, thank you for understanding. It is greatly appreciated. Take care out there.

Are you on better terms with anyone in your life than you used to be? Does it feel better not to feel hatred swell up inside of you with the mere mention of that person's name? Is it not nice to have one less worry in our day-to-day lives? We must learn to let go of our negative emotions toward others-not only for them, but also for ourselves. It can help us out in many ways. It could possibly help us in ways we could not have imagined.

> "Any man may easily do harm, but not every man can
> do good to another."
> —Plato

The other exemplary story involving my experiences with hatred is one that is in a completely different phase of progression. This story is about a girl I once dated, and how I struggle with letting go of my resentment for her, even now.

I dated this girl over the summer of 2009, and I am ashamed of it now. I should not have dated her in the first place; she had already shown signs of bad character that I chose to ignore. The lies and deceit had already been apparent, and I should have known better. I did it anyway, disappointing some of my close friends in the process. She played the victim role very well and had me thinking she was a vulnerable and scared individual who was so unsure of her life. And oh, what a good actress she was.

We broke up around the four-month mark, and I did not care to see her ever again. I had deemed her untrustworthy, felt like she never cared for the relationship we shared as much as I did and like she did not try to help make any of our issues better. She was too apathetic about everything for me, and she just was not what I wanted from a girlfriend.

I did not trust her because of situations involving three different guys that happened while we were dating. She had an ex-boyfriend who she still hung out with a lot, a dance partner that she practiced for her dance competitions with, and I felt like she liked one of my close friends at the time, but she denied liking him the entire time. I ended up finding out from two different reliable sources that she had been cheating on me with both her ex-boyfriend and her "dance partner," and additionally, she did indeed have the feelings for my friend that she had so boldly denied. My concerns were all justified, but unfortunately, that is nowhere near the end of it.

I found out later that she had never even told her ex-boyfriend that she had a boyfriend the entire time that we were dating. She led him on the entire time, letting him believe that she was single. She acted upon her falsely-presented single status with him and on many occasions. After learning about this entire ordeal, I contacted him out of curiosity and asked him a few questions. He confirmed what I already knew and apologized. She always made him out to be some horrible person. They supposedly did not have contact with each other anymore, but she was playing us all.

Furthermore, she never had a dance competition and it was all made up. This other guy *was* in her dance class, but there were no *dance practices* between them for any *competition*. No late-evening rehearsals with the team. I originally split with her because of completely unrelated reasons, and then I found out all of this out weeks after the fact. What a bombshell.

A few weeks after finding all this out, I was asked by a few people I hardly knew if I had ever physically hurt this girl. They also asked me if a few other sinister allegations were true. None of them were. She had spread rumors about heinous things I supposedly had done to her while we were dating and told people how "horrible" I was to her. She went after my dignity, and it was all maliciously out of spite. The night I broke up with her, she had begged for me not to leave. She told me that I was the one who had always treated her best. She cried so hard. That was all probably just a lie, as well.

Looking back on everything, I honestly do not know if she ever told me a single truth.

Another factor of duality in her plague upon my mental security was how I saw myself become another lie along her path of deceit. She had told me horror stories about her other ex-boyfriends. She had told me how mistreated she always seemed to be, and how unfair her relationships always turned out to be. Now I was the next "ex-boyfriend who had been so hurtful and abusive" toward her. I had become another lie that would fuel her fire of explosive self-pity. She could add my name to her line up for people she could falsely rant about to future boyfriends. Maybe even, one day, her misguided husband.

People had heard negative things about how I had treated her, what I did and said to her, and they found her to be the victim. People had no reason not to believe her immediately. After all, I had previously fallen for her deceit just as easily. But I knew how she truly felt in the midst of all this. I knew what was going on. On top of all the hearsay, she had cheated on me with two different guys, and she was involved with one of them the entire time we dated. She ended up dating that friend of mine whom I suspected that she liked while we were dating. She later cheated on him, too.

After all of these events had happened, and I thought our situation was all over, I was surprised once again. She lied to and manipulated one of my friends I had known since the age of seven. After twelve years of friendship, he decided I was a horrible person, a man who was apparently unworthy of a girl as good as this one. He believed the things she told him, the ammunition that she whispered in his ear, the fingers she pointed at me. He and I had been naturally drifting apart due to differences, but this was the gavel coming down on the judge's bench. And she was the judge in session.

Even as I write this, I get antsy. I want to let loose and just start ranting on about her. Like I said before, I am trying to overcome these feelings, but it is not easy. She haunted my social life for many months, and took advantage of me countless times. It agitates me to think about. Those memories elicit frustration and disgust and are laced with hate. When I am able to let the negative feelings go, I will feel much better. I will need to forgive her and somehow try to accept how she rendered me tattered and hurt. I need to do so for my own sake.

> "We are products of our past, but we do not have to be prisoners of it."
>
> —Rick Warren

My stories are probably not too different from many others out there. Most of us probably have something like this happening right now. Reading this chapter, you have almost certainly thought of someone in your own mind that you struggle to forgive. Someone who walked on you. Someone who hurt you. Someone who cut you down inside. We just need to get the poison out of our heads.

It may seem cliché, but we must learn to forgive people; everyone. We do not have to be friendly to these people. They do not have to be our friends, and we do not have to associate with them on a daily basis. But we cannot brew hateful feelings about people and expect for it to make us feel more free or happy. It will be hard, but we must try. We must all try together.

Letting go of hard feelings from our past can ultimately let us move forward and better ourselves. We can combine these actions with the themes from *Learn from Your Mistakes*. Use these feelings, not for harboring, but for learning. Harbor joy and the good memories that will allow us to laugh and smile together. We can reminisce about the better times in life. Let us try not to harbor anger and hatred, for they do no one any good.

Maybe we can move past those partly cloudy days and open our hearts to better experiences. Perhaps we should not focus on the partly cloudy skies, but instead simply enjoy the sunshine in between.

Some might say that forgiving people for these kinds of things just lets it happen again. Some may say that it just shows that we do not stand up for ourselves. Forgiveness does not mean that we will just sit around and let it happen to us again. We simply try to relate with others, attempt to understand why they may have committed certain acts, and not to hate them for what they have done. We can still stand up for ourselves involving those people or situations, and I would encourage it. But try not to harbor constantly plaguing and hateful feelings and wishes. It sours the soul. I saw the positive results with Justin when I dropped the resentment and moved on. Maybe we all can.

CONFRONT YOUR WEAKNESSES

Yeah, we all have them. Even you and I. Inside our heads and throughout our reflective thoughts, we are aware of at least a few of our weaknesses. Now we just have to admit their existence.

Take a second while you begin to read about this Pillar and think about your weaknesses. What are they, how do you think they came to be, and how does it affect you? Even better, how do these weaknesses affect the ones around you? Hopefully your answer was not one denying the existence of any weaknesses. Letting go of denial is the first stage for some to admit that we have flaws in life. Imperfections can make us feel vulnerable, yet these qualities simply make us human.

In a sense, this Pillar is all about honesty. Being honest deals not only with our interactions with others, but also with ourselves. It is very easy to lie to yourself. People do it every day. Denying that we do not have any weaknesses is a façade and just an illusion to our own eyes. Stopping this trickery and being truthful to ourselves about our own personality is the first step, and they say the first step is always the hardest.

After we have admitted that we have weaknesses or flaws, then it is time to keep something in mind. We must always remember that our shortcomings do not mean we are broken. It does not make us unworthy or unfit for society. We all have certain character traits that will flare up less-than-perfect situations in life, but that does not make us unworthy.

With that said, we all know there are different levels of flaws out there. If it is something that can easily be helped, maybe we should work on that flaw as soon as possible. There is a difference in being severely overweight and living in denial vs. recognizing that something must be done.

Weaknesses are often social or personal traits that embarrass or frustrate us about ourselves, and admitting them first is crucial so that we can then deal with them. In the Pillar *Hold the Diamonds of Others,* I admit that I have a problem with letting one person's flaw corrupt my whole image of them. In *Harbor Love Not Hate* I admit that I have a hard time letting go of hating people who have severely wronged me. In *Hold Respect for Others* I elaborate on how I can be very disrespectful and hateful toward my father. These weaknesses are no less a part of who I am than my own genetic codes. The same is true for all of us. Our flaws are a part of what makes us unique and what gives us identity. I feel like ignoring these things is the worst thing that we could do, and I feel like we should never just leave them alone.

> "The greatest weakness of all is the great fear of appearing weak."
>
> —Jacques Benique Bossuel

Throughout this book I mention several weaknesses of mine that I have attempted to mend over time. In addition to those mentioned, I will elaborate on another weakness of mine, and one that frustrates me to no end. This would happen to be my minor speech anxiety that I developed in Middle School, and how I have dealt with that since then. I realize it may be a pretty low-key, common weakness compared to some others out there, but perhaps this is one that people can relate to.

I remember it very clearly, and I even remember where I was sitting in the room at the time. There was a substitute teacher that day. It was eighth grade history class, and we were all taking turns reading three paragraphs from our history book. Trust me. This was the most exciting and engaging activity in all of my schooling.

We had done this type of reading activity several times before, but little did I know that this time would be different. When it was my turn to read I started without hesitation. I began noticing my voice shaking while I was reading the first paragraph, which triggered my brain to stop focusing on reading and instead on how nervous I had suddenly become. I did not even have time to question why.

I could not even register the words I was reading. My face and ears got hot, my eyes started watering, and I could hardly catch my breath. My heart was racing a marathon and I began baking in my own skin. I could not even audibly speak to keep reading, and it sounded like I was hyperventilating. If you did not know any better, you would have thought by the sound of it that I had started crying while I was reading. The kid in front of me turned around to witness the breakdown that was happening behind him, and I could not even look up from the page that I was so desperately scrambling to read. I will never be able to forget that specific feeling of utter shame and embarrassment.

The substitute teacher looked at me in curiosity and she asked for the next kid after me to start reading where I had stopped. I was not even completely through the second paragraph. Words cannot describe the feeling and emotions that were drowning me. Why had I freaked out? Why could I not even read three paragraphs from a book? There were only thirty people in my class. Thirty. People give speeches to crowds of thousands upon thousands. And this kid could not even read his book for thirty people. I felt lower than the carpeted floor my desk was sitting on; walked on by my own psyche.

Here is where the sheer mentality of this weakness kicks in. I started severely overreacting about any form of talking for a group and feared speaking out loud in a class at all. I remember in one of my classes in tenth grade, the same reading activity was happening, and my turn was about to come around. We had three slips we could use that would allow us to go to the bathroom during class and not get in trouble, and I used one to avoid having to read. I just sat in the stall long enough for my turn to undoubtedly have passed. In one of my ninth grade classes we would all answer short answer questions out loud from our worksheets. I would count ahead, see what mine was going to be, and find ways to shorten my oral answer and rehearse it before my turn came. It became a constant worry and dread that never left me alone.

This seeped into my social life as well. I remember being at a church when I was in ninth grade with a girlfriend of mine. We were all taking turns reading a paragraph of scripture in small groups of six. I tried to skip my turn but instead read aloud, and barely hop-skipped-and-jumped my way through the section. I had freaked out and worked myself up in a circle of six kids. This weakness was beginning to consume me.

This process and worry has followed me through the years, even to today. This haunting never seems to let go of me. Every time I ever escalate with fear and dread over speaking in these situations, I become embarrassed and ashamed. I know what I am feeling is silly and not justified. It seems to overpower me, and eat at my thoughts; my rationality.

With that being said, I am happy to say the situation has gotten a lot better. It starts with my personality. Back in eighth grade, I was the quiet and shy kid that never spoke up unless spoken to first. Now I find myself to be very social and outgoing. The fear of having to say a sentence or two in front of a class slowly and painfully went away in my first two years of college. It took dozens and dozens of situations to slowly warm me up to handling talking in front of large groups. Oral presentations still give me hell, but things have alleviated so much from that infamous day back in eighth grade.

Here is where the mentality of this thing does not let go. My complete persona has changed over the years, but that fear has not. People are so surprised when they hear that I have this deeply embedded concern because they find me to be outgoing and I seem to be such a people-person. In my head though, anytime I hear the word "presentation," my heart skips a beat, and my stomach turns a bit. I wish it were different and I hate that I fear it so much. This is such an overreaction and mental chess game I put myself through, and it is one of my biggest hang-ups in my opinion.

I always tell myself that if I fixed my speech anxiety, I would enjoy my classes twice as much. It is always my answer when asked about my biggest thing that I do not like about myself. Knowing I have a speech the next week can stress me out more than any test I have ever sat down to take. I lose my appetite for the entire day of the actual presentation, and it consumes every minute of thought. But, when it is all said and done, I feel like a car has been lifted from my shoulders. I feel rejuvenated.

Since arriving at OSU, I have had a few presentations and they have surprised me. I seem to be getting better at controlling my sort of "panic attacks" during my presentations, and I am able to keep talking and slowly push forward. I dread them from the time I hear about them, worry the entire time, and then breathe the biggest sigh of relief after it is over with. Sometimes I will just sit in my room, stomach in knots, and cry out of frustration right before a big presentation. The whole thing overwhelms me, and I know it should not be a big deal. This sense of speech anxiety is the crow that picks at my liver as I, a social Prometheus, am chained to a rock.

I have been asked to be the best man at two of my best friends' weddings this next year. The two ceremonies are a week apart from one another, and I find myself nervous and tense when thinking about delivering those two speeches in front of crowds topping one-hundred. Worrying about a minute-long speech a year away seems so pitiful. Trust me, I know. But that is how far this flaw embeds itself under my skin and in my brain. I hope to be a lot better at public speaking by that time, and I will hopefully be able to deliver an amazing couple of speeches for two very important days in my friends' lives. It should be all about them, not me.

> "Growth begins when we begin to accept our own weakness."
>
> —Jean Vanier

As I write this, I have a presentation coming up for a job interview that I am dreading and getting very nervous about. Hopefully it folds out as well as the others have been lately. I think about it daily and worry about it twice as much. I can lead a film club of twenty-five as president or talk to my residence hall floor of fifty guys, but I cannot get up in a suit in front of people and just talk for a few minutes. Something about it just unravels me into threads. It is a very frustrating weakness, and one I feel like I should be able to help; especially by this time in my life. I will continue to work on it, though. I will speak up more in class, and try to face these presentations head on with shimmering confidence. Ignorance and avoidance of the issue does nothing but burrow the splinter even deeper.

What I will say about this fear is that it has led me to other forms of expression. I think that may be why I love writing and filmmaking so much. I find it easier to express myself and to relate my thoughts. Things never flow like Shakespeare when I am so nervous that I may faint, but in other mediums everything can be refined and executed in a more collected manner. It may have opened doors for me to use, but at the same time, I cannot help but see it as also dodging the bullet.

Another weakness that seems to slither its way into situations I encounter is my lack of communication. Often times, this involves me getting mad at others for something, but not ever communicating it very well to that specific person. When I get frustrated or mad I just get quiet and stop talking or elaborating. This does not really solve problems or move things along, but it is what I seem to end up doing time and time again.

Sometimes I will even get mad at people for something that just ends up being an issue of poor communication. I will find myself expecting people to have magically figured something out by themselves. This happens for many reasons, but sometimes it occurs because of some lack of communication that I failed to relay to them. This ends up causing the gap between our mindsets. Then, I get frustrated and shut down, and it only widens the communication gap even further. The chasm is only dug deeper.

What I have to do is see that I have the tendency to do this sort of thing, and try to counter it as or before it happens. If I can realize it is an issue that may pop up again, then I can look for it in my arguments and disagreements that I have with others. Just like speaking in front of people, this occasional gap of communication will be something I will face and continue to work on.

Dealing with our weaknesses is a step ahead and one we should definitely be taking. Admitting those weaknesses first is more important and it allows for us to realize we are, after all, only human. Many people never want to appear weak at all, or in any way. This happens a lot in a group of guys. What are we hiding from, though? There is no shame in being yourself and truly allowing others to know the real you.

Your weaknesses are just as much of a part of you as your laugh or smile. It is what makes you . . . well, you. So, admit them. Let them fly, and then work with them. Use that to better yourself for the future. Things can only haunt you when you run from them, so stand and fight. Show us who you really are, flaws and all.

STAY AT FACE VALUE

Why do status symbols even exist? These possessions are nothing more than products made to showcase one's wealth or social status. Besides the obvious fact that these are products made for us to showcase how much money we may or may not have, truly ask yourself: why would we endorse such a thing? I feel like we should not buy things just to try and have others find us wealthy. The things we buy and own, as well as the things we do, should be solely . . . for us.

It may seem like a simple answer, or like it was a dumb question to ask in the first place, but it is the truth. This is something I feel like we do not pay enough detailed attention to. We buy plenty of things to try and impress others or just to fit in. We want them to find us attractive, wealthy, pampered, stylish, or maybe even cool. Everyone has the natural tendency to want to be liked, but it becomes a topic of concern when people spend more money on a lavish outfit or a new face-lift than they did on their vehicle parked out in the driveway.

> "You may not control all the events that happen to you,
> but you can decide not to be reduced by them."
> —Maya Angelou

In marketing and psychology, this trend is known as *conspicuous consumption*. This type of spending is meant to display one's wealth or social status, and not really much else. It rolls into spending our own money just to try and to show others how much we are able to spend. I do not think we should feel a need to try and cause envy in others, and I feel like we should just focus on ourselves. Envy is a feeling, desire, and an emotion that leads down a bad road. It does not seem to do anything positive for anybody.

Children are always told to not worry about impressing others, or showing off, but rather to just live for themselves. As we hand down such advice to children, I think we can very often lose sight of the values ourselves. There is a concept that I think could transform the way we think about the things we buy and how we spend money. Instead of consuming conspicuously or buying status symbols, we could stick to a different rule of thumb. What if we bought things based on who we are, not who we wanted to be seen as?

We all remember coming home as kids and asking our parents to buy us something because other kids had it. Is it not odd that the same spending desires transpire into our adulthoods? What about that desire carries all the way with us through the years? The desire to be noticed by someone? The inner need for acceptance? Sometimes, instead of being driven by our own expression, we go off what we think society tells us is cool. That seems a lot like being led into the dark by a person who is blindfolded.

I was a little guy, ten years old and in fifth grade to be exact, and I wanted to dress *cooler.* I had noticed that the popular kids at my elementary school had been wearing these certain types of over shirts. Most of these over shirts had dragon print on them and were bright colors, while the undershirt was often white and black. As I write this, I cannot help but wonder why I remember this so well. It probably has something to do with the fact that so much emotion was involved in such activities; the pursuit to be heralded as *cool* or *elite.* The urge to spend money on such a feeling can become overpowering, as we have seen all around us.

As we transferred into the sixth grade, and our elementary school fused with six others under the roof of the Owasso Sixth Grade Center, the dressing fads changed very quickly, as fads tend to do. I did not keep up, however, and got left behind. I remember being made fun of by a kid one day for wearing my purple over shirt. It was no longer cool, and I no longer wanted these shirts at all. I could care less about them, and I was now upset. It was at this time I remember being so mad about what I had done.

Since then, I try to dress and buy things just for me. I have my band shirts that express my favorite music, and other clothes that I bought because I like the colors, or the designs. I try to always remember that everything we do day in and day out is an extension or who we are. Expression cannot get basic enough, because in essence, anything that we do from an idle mind is wasted. Keeping purpose, even in our possessions, can speak volumes about who we are.

Since I have become a student here at OSU, I have noticed a lot of trends that are driven by minor status symbols. These items may all have different origins, but they have all risen into the same pool of products. Many people say they like these products because they are of high quality. We have to ask ourselves when half of a college campus is wearing the same five brands from head to toe, when does the trend start becoming *conspicuous* (in reference to conspicuous consumption)? Sperry, Ray-Ban, Polo, Nike, and North Face. Each item has its own forte, but these five brands could claim half of the clothing market here at OSU. I am not saying that anyone who has ever worn any of these things did it because everyone else was, but somewhere along the way, someone hopped on some form of bandwagon.

> "Be yourself; everyone else is already taken."
> —Oscar Wilde

I have seen these effects myself first hand. I have had talks with friends who complained about such trends and how it makes everyone look the exact same on campus. Weeks later, the same friend came in wearing these things that they had previously said were dumb to buy. I have done this before myself. In fact, as I write this, I am wearing my pair of Nike shoes. Perhaps we get tired of not fitting in, and decide we want to be part of the trend. We all want to find our fit into the puzzle of life, but sometimes when others around us jam our piece into certain slots, regardless of the fit, we should insist on knowing why.

This topic includes more than just status symbols and people buying things to try and seem cool or wealthy. Staying at face value also speaks volumes about what we do and say on a daily basis. From big story-telling about heavily-fabricated memories to doing certain activities just to try and fit in, there are a lot of things we do in the wake of outside sources. For instance, I have a friend of mine whose stories now fall on deaf ears. People do not care to listen to his stories anymore because there are always inconsistencies and fake information. A classic example of the boy who cried wolf.

The more frequently we are not sincere in the things we buy and do, the less people are going to believe that any of these actions are for ourselves. They just might start assuming we are doing everything based on what we think is popular, or what makes us seem wealthy. We all want to be liked and accepted, but we can do that by being ourselves. If we lie to everyone we meet by not really doing things for the right reasons, then what kind of first impressions are we trying to make? The sands that shift for anything are able to hold nothing.

There are so many pressures in today's world to be attractive, cool, or trendy and it drives peoples' lives. Modern advertising does nothing but play on our emotions and deep desires to be accepted and cherished. A lot of campaigns try to make us think that the more money we earn annually, the more *successful* we are. These pressures can take the reins of our own decisions and strand us in the middle of nowhere. The more we let others drive our lives, the less we are getting to live our own. I think we can all agree that we would like to have more of our lives in our own hands. So please, be my guest.

Remember in the cliché high school movies when the jocks would make fun of the gothic kids because they dressed differently? The reality might not be as cheesy or easy to see in reality, but things like that happen every day, and in many places. This is something we cannot fear, though. Staying at face value is like the Pillar, *Criticism Comes from Solidity,* but with a focus on our appearance and how we relate ourselves to other people. From the car you drive to the shirt on your back, do it for you, and not because someone over there did it too. Then we can all be different. Together.

"To be yourself in a world that is constantly trying to make you something else is the greatest accomplishment."
                                        —Ralph Waldo Emerson

In essence, this chapter pleas for everyone to just be themselves. We would not want to just, as some aptly say, "Drink the kool-aid." "Kool-aid" produced by those who relish telling us what to do. Whether this involves how we dress, act, feel, talk, or who you hang around, other people's expectations should not drive our lives. We should take the steering wheel in our own hands, and take the roads we want to. The highway may be where everyone else is driving, but maybe your destination is nowhere near theirs. Perhaps the back roads were made just for you.

LEARN FROM YOUR MISTAKES

Living with no regrets is a way of life for many. Some people advise not to look back on life and only push forward. In certain situations, those words of advice can be very valuable. But if we live with no regrets and do not look back at our past at all, what are we supposed to do about those errors we've already made? None of us are perfect, so there will always be lessons to learn along the way, often through the mistakes that we have made in life. How about a healthy medium between the two? What if we choose not to live in sulking regret but remember our mistakes, using them for our own betterment? What if we used the memories of our mistakes and utilized them for our future?

A situation happened in front of me while writing this book that reminded me of this Pillar. One of my close friends was cleaning off her island counter in the kitchen after dinner. As she wiped the counter, she bumped her candle warmer and it spilled melted wax over all over the table. I watched in slight horror as warm fluid splashed across the counter. Luckily the candle was not too large, and not too much molten candle wax was spilled. I figured the candle was done, that it had been ruined. Then she did something that I had not thought of, for some reason: she waited a minute to clean up the mess, and then started scraping the spilt wax up. It had hardened after being cooled back down. She then took all the wax in her hand and dropped it back into the hot candle. It quickly re-warmed and melted back in with the rest of the leftover wax. She recovered every bit of the accident. This little, yet simple, situation reflects on our past and our mistakes. We can discard them, or we could utilize them to live on and rejuvenate everything that lies ahead. It just depends on how you look at everything.

> "Be not ashamed of mistakes and thus make them crimes."
>
> —Confucius

We have all made mistakes. Many of us have things we have done before, that if given the opportunity, we would try to change. Some of us wish we could go back in time and be given a second chance to redo something from our past. Some of us are saddened to see how some situations have unfolded. Could we not turn each of these thoughts and feelings into valuable lessons that could better prepare us for the future? Our past is a major part of who we are, and it is a valuable thing to be able to harness. Why not use that to our advantage?

People often say that the best lessons in life are those learned the hard way. To me, that means our mistakes and the tribulations we face in life that challenge us end up being the most valuable. We just have to keep in mind that we have the possibility to pull these lessons from our past and be wiser as we move forward. Think about a mistake you have made in life, or about things that you have done that you regret. Think about things that other people might say you regret. What has that taught you about life and about yourself?

This book is full of mistakes from my past. We all have a list of our mistakes that grows as the sun rises and falls each day, because as we know so well, no one is perfect. I try to take a lesson from each and every mistake I make in life, no matter how insignificant or gigantic. Some of the mistakes that I find to be the biggest thus far in my life are elaborated on in other Pillars of the book. So in light of this Pillar, I will just mention several mistakes and lessons in life that have taught me a thing or two. Perhaps this is why we consider our elders to be so wise; because they have seen many more mistakes and have had many more chances to learn from life itself.

Relationships are a sector of life that can carry this Pillar single-handedly. This does not mean relationships that do not last are a mistake, but they are definitely something to learn from. Each relationship we encounter and experience in life teaches us so much about what we adore in another person. Those relationships that come to an end teach us more about what we may or may not want from the next situation that we involve ourselves in. Look at it like a set of stepping stones laid out through a garden. Each experience is a progression from the previous stone, allowing for the next step to be taken. Then, at any point in life, we can turn around and see the winding stepping stones we have traveled and see just exactly how and why we ended up where we are now.

Any person that we grow close to can tell us something about ourselves and teach us a lesson. The good situations show us the enriching qualities we will look for in another person and the characteristics we value in a personal relationship. The negative situations, and most often the things that cause the fall-outs, are the observations that can keep us from repeating a bad history, like bumpers on a bowling lane. I tend to see it this like this: the more we experience and learn from our mistakes in life, the further our bumpers extend down our lane and keep our ball from diverging into the gutter. At that point, it is only our personal fulfillment—those ten unsuspecting pins—which lay ahead.

> "Experience is the name everyone gives to their mistakes."
>
> —Oscar Wilde

Most of us have pets, and many of us love them like family—good family. My parents and I had a dog named Rocky when I was younger. He was a boxer-pit-bull mix, and when he came home with my mom he was no bigger than a Barbie doll and was downright adorable. As he got older, he got much bigger, and howled in fear and angst the first few nights he had to stay outside, which was both sad and adorable. As time went on, however, and as he grew larger, his extreme amount of energy and power became an annoying force to be reckoned with. He frequently pushed friends and family down, tripped people over, and was completely relentless to anyone who tried to come in our yard. I started not to like the dog.

Do not get me wrong; I love dogs. I also adore cats, for that matter. He had his days where he would sit and I could pet him without being mauled in a fever of energy. Those days came few and far between. I guess it got to a point where I gave up on him, and decided not to give him any more attention because of it. It got to a point where I did not like him at all anymore.

I was at a get-together with people from work on a sunny afternoon in May of 2009 when I got a phone call from my dad. He told me that Rocky was dead, and that he was sorry. We had an old Indian-paint pony out in our pasture by the name of Patchy, and Rocky had escaped our yard earlier in the day. Rocky ended up in the pasture with our pony, and his canine instincts took over. He was running down, and practically hunting, our elderly and innocent horse. My dad tried to stop everything without any violent force, but Rocky had torn giant pieces of flesh from Patchy's front quarters. There was only one way to stop him by that point. My dad took his gun and shot Rocky, ending his life immediately in order to save Patchy.

As I listened to the story over the phone, I was surprised at the hot tears cascading down my cheeks. I was mourning a dog that I had grown to dislike (or so I thought). After getting off the phone with my dad, I cried some more. I could not help the sinking guilt and regret of never having treated him better than I had. I wished I had been more grateful and loving to a loyal pal of mine. Even though he had to be killed for what he was doing, it was still very tragic and sad. I make a note to love on both my dogs I have now, Reno and Chico, and give them at least a little of my adoration each day. My ferret I'd had since seventh grade died last summer, and that was very difficult for me to deal with. When she passed, I knew I had given her my affection, and that she had lived a good life. At least I could take comfort in that.

> "An expert is a person who has made all the mistakes that can be made in a very narrow field."
>
> —Niels Bohr

Learning from our mistakes is just like the classic situation of a child touching the hot stove. When you touch the hot burner and burn your finger, you learn not to touch that surface again when it happens to be glowing red. We do not want to touch the hot burner again because of its consequences and what we endured the last time we did such a thing. Our other mistakes in life are no different and can be used just as aptly.

For instance, as a little tyke, I once had a severe case of poison ivy and was more than uncomfortable for days. I had gone against my parents' simple advice on how to prevent such a plague. I quickly learned how to prevent involving my bare skin with poison ivy, what it looked like, and how to avoid even getting near it.

Poison ivy is a lot like our mistakes. If we repeat our same blunders and get into poison ivy time and time again, the rash reappears. Muddle within that situation, scratch your rash a little bit, and it quickly spreads. The itching is unforgiving and can end up making our life hellacious. Learn from the infectious consequences, do not allow for them to spread, and harvest the life lessons. If we learn from enough mistakes, we could walk through an enormous jungle of poison ivy without even being scathed. When we arm ourselves to be protected from head to toe, we are practically untouchable.

When a teenager begins to get their first paychecks from their first job, it is a brand new experience, and often an exciting time. For the first time, that adolescent earned money for themselves and has disposable income from their hard work. When I was in this phase of life, I learned a very important lesson from a mistake of mine. A paycheck that was over $200 was spent in one week . . . on food. From Sonic to Taco Bell, I spent it all. I could not even believe it. My mind could not wrap around the idea that I had just blown my entire paycheck on food. Needless to say, that was a quick wake-up call, and I have watched my income more closely ever since. It is better to waste a few first paychecks than years of my self-earned money. Learning from our mistakes has its benefits, in an endless amount of ways.

This is one of those practices that seems to grow easier over time, and learning from our mistakes is no different than a deathly-trained warrior. The more times that the stubborn boy gets up and recovers from being beaten, the tougher and more prepared he is for the next fight. So please, do not let your mistakes whip you to the floor. Stand up and keep those same mistakes from happening again. Cover those scars, use them to make you stronger, and fight on. Hoorah.

EMPATHY NOT ENVY

Empathy is not linked with envy too often, unless someone is trying to rhyme the two. But they are connected in how we react to certain feelings and experiences. There are a lot of things that can cause us to be envious of another person and it rarely leads to good things. Envy is a feeling that could be lived without, and as discussed in *Stay at Face Value*, envy is not a pleasant thing to lie onto others. Dealing with it from the other side of the fence is another challenge in itself.

Like I said, we can get envious of others for a multitude of reasons, many of which lead to anger or resentment. Envy can stem from witnessing others' family life, social status, economic positions, possessions, genetics, and many other parts of a person's mantra. Most of the time envy seeps in when we see someone who has something that we wish we had, for whatever reason. Empathy has the potential to come in full swing here, sweep us off our feet, and remind us of the bigger picture.

Empathy, the ability to identify well with others' life experiences, can help us through all walks of life. From our friendships and parental relationships to how we conduct ourselves with the other people in our careers, empathy is a powerful tool in today's world. Everyone is looking for some sort of sincere connection, whether it is at home, the gym, the grocery store, or the office. We love to be around people who genuinely care about us, and empathy is the catalyst for such a reaction to take place. We just have to remember when to pour it in.

"Resentment is like drinking poison and waiting for the other person to die."

—Carrie Fisher

So where does envy and empathy come together and form some sort of decisional relation? It begins with envy. For me, this is one of the Pillars that I have a lot of trouble with. I tend to deal with this kind of frustration pretty frequently, and I need to keep empathy within my arms' reach. I think that we all need to remember that we are not complete controllers of our fates in this unruly world.

This story is one that took place over the summer during writing this book. I was supposed to go on a date with a friend of a friend, and I was supposed to pick her up. I was nervous because I had not gone on any sort of date in a while, but I was also excited. I had been told that I would like her house, and that she was pretty "well off." When she told me the neighborhood that she lived in, I knew her family was not, well, struggling to make ends meet, you could say.

As I pulled up to the house, I was astounded. Their garage was contending to have more floor space than my entire house; in all seriousness. I wondered if I should park my car outside of their moat or not, because this thing looked like a castle. I was floored, and hesitated a second before stepping out of my car to approach the front door. I felt like I was about to walk out onto a stage, with judging eyes zeroed in on me.

She, and a big dog of hers, greeted me at the door and she invited me in for a second. As I walked in, I could not help but feel like I was the camera man about to shoot for MTV Cribs. This place was immaculate. I almost expected a butler to approach me or for one of those bear rugs with the head still attached to be laying over in the living room. I tried not to judge these people by the size of their home—never judge a book by its cover, right? But this was one heck of a book cover.

As we were leaving, I opened my car door for her as I contemplated how many times her parents' income could run circles around my parents'. I knew that this way of thinking was not good, but I could not help it. Facing extreme opposites from our own lives is not an everyday experience. We then proceeded to go to dinner together at my favorite restaurant in Tulsa. I wondered what she thought of my car, or of my favorite restaurant, or of me in general.

After dinner I brought her back to her house, and she asked if I wanted to see her dad's cars. She knew I liked cars and thought I'd be interested. I happily obliged and was impressed when I laid my eyes upon two different Porsches. One of them was being built from scratch. I was also surprised to see a complete shop's worth of amazing tools, as well as a fully transportable and functioning car lift. From a car-guy's perspective, envy erupted into jealousy-ridden volcanic ash. This setup was amazing and to die for.

On top of that, I got a tour of the entire castle, and was just in awe when comparing what I had grown up with compared to all of this. I had grown up in a small log cabin in a rural part of town, so in contrast, this was a *castle*. I also got to meet her siblings and parents as we strolled back through the house. As I walked out that night I felt smaller than a pin drop. Getting into my car, and leaving the neighborhood, all I could think about was the incredible array of possessions and monetary power I had just witnessed. Envy, laced with frustration, drove me home that night.

I was frustrated, felt incredibly inferior, and feared a day when someone like that, or even her, asked to come and see my place. These were misplaced emotions, but they occurred because I was in a mini state of shock. I had not really been around a house like that before, especially not one belonging to a girl that I was now going on a first date with. First impressions are everything, but I needed to slow way down.

Envy was bullying me into a chain-linked corner on the playground, but here is where empathy decided to come over and give me a helping hand. When in situations of envy and frustration, we have to ask ourselves why we are reacting to such a thing. I was just reacting this way based on my own life and experiences. I was viewing it through only one person's perspective: mine. I needed to step back and realize a few things.

For starters, she did not ask to be born into such a situation. She did not ask to be placed in such a nicely padded lifestyle, it just ended up happening that way. On top of that, she was not as rich as she could be. Her dad could have had 20 cars, or many more, like Jay Leno. She could have been driving some luxury car that she did not care about, but instead she was driving a regular car, which she did care for. She did not complain about it either.

Their house could have been bigger, and the whole family could have been snobby. They could have acted like they were celebrities and only let the rich and famous into their home. When it came down to it, she and her family were all very nice, genuine, and very polite people. Nobody even asked me what my parents did for a living, which is what my dad would have asked. That is just because he is nosy, though.

She never asked me how much my parents made, how big my savings account may have been, and over our next outing or so, I discovered that she did something that most people in positions like her do not do: she tried to downplay her socioeconomic status. She did not like talking about her house or how much money her family made. Later on in our friendship (we decided to just be friends for a handful of unrelated reasons), she talked about how much privilege she realizes she has gotten to take a part in, and she knows how life is for others. In summary, this young lady was so humble that if you did not already know it, you may have never guessed what kind of lifestyle she had come from.

> "Envy is the most stupid of vices, for there is no single advantage to be gained from it."
> —Honore de Balzac

As I realized more and more that the feelings I had that first night were misplaced, I started thinking about a concept that made me feel even smaller than when I was leaving her house. I imagined a different, and opposite scenario.

What if I had picked a girl up in the exact opposite position? What if she was from an intensely poor neighborhood, had nothing even close to what I had the privilege of growing up with, and asked to come over to see my house? My heart would have sunk, because

I would have realized then and there, how things truly tasted on the other side of the fence.

Empathy involves letting go of our own biases and judgments, and stepping into someone else's shoes, no matter the size. It entails understanding other people, where they come from, why they believe and act how they do, and in a real sense, giving them a fair chance. This girl, now a friend of mine, did not care about money or possessions that first night we went to dinner. She just wanted to hang out with me and enjoy my company (imagine that, right?). Envy does nothing but ruin possible relationships between people and sour otherwise positive attitudes. It paves a one way negative street that leads nowhere good.

Empathize with people you meet and know in life. From young children, to your peers who disagree with you. The more patience and fairness you deal out the more empathetic you can become. In the business world, empathy is becoming a buzzword, and people are starting to treasure these kinds of traits on and off the time clock. Empathy, for lack of a better word, is truly and honestly caring. No fake smile. It is sitting yourself down, and offering true and undivided sincerity to another person.

> "Love looks through a telescope; envy, through a microscope."
>
> —Josh Billings

The people in your life that you enjoy venting to have a knack for being empathetic. They keep eye contact, give you direct feedback, and do not pay any attention to anything but you and what you are saying. You can tell, just by their attentive silence, that they truly care. Without a friend or person like that, people have nowhere to go for personal relief. These people can take a stressful day off in seconds and have you feeling loved and smiling in a minute flat. Why would we not be that person for the ones we love? Guess how valuable people in life like that are.

Let us try to overcome envy, you and I. Like I said earlier, replacing envy with empathy is something I myself need to work on. I find myself very quick to get agitated at those who are rich, famous, privileged, and wealthy. Then again, I personally know people who brag more about what they make or have than those who are actually rich or wealthy. But one thing I need to keep in mind is this: I only think in these patterns because of the way I came to be. What if I was them? How would I want Ivan to think of me then? Perhaps with some empathy, not envy; no rhyme intended.

IT IS ALL ABOUT
WHAT YOU DO

Words and actions make up your footprint
on this planet, and there is a limitless amount of ways
you could go about it. How will you sculpt your life
and the legacy you leave behind?

Be Entrepreneurial

No, this chapter is not recommending you to jump out and start your own business. In the Entrepreneurship School of OSU, the act of entrepreneurship is loosely defined as: *the process of creating value by bringing together a unique combination of resources to exploit an opportunity.* The common mistake people make with the word *entrepreneurship* is they assume it means owning your own business. Although it often times *does* mean starting and owning a new business venture, being entrepreneurial can transfer into a multitude of things. I could choose to eat or dress entrepreneurially if I wanted. *How so* you may ask.

> "Action is the foundational key to all success."
> —Pablo Picasso

There are five aspects to being entrepreneurial. In essence, entrepreneurship can be broken down to a process. The thing about processes is that they than can be replicated, taught, and be transferred to other areas. First, the person involved needs to be proactive, and in junction with that be very observant of the world around them. Secondly, there needs to be an opportunity that can be taken advantage of. Next, there is a value proposition, or the idea used to exploit an opportunity. Then comes the unique set of resources to do such a thing, and the execution plan to get it all done.

It is easy to see how this process can be used to turn an idea or invention into a working business that operates and serves customers.

On the other side of the coin, it is also recognizable how these aspects could be reflected onto many other things in life. But right now, you are probably asking yourself: *I get that it is not just owning your own business, by what does he mean by "being entrepreneurial" in my life?* To me, being entrepreneurial means changing the world one baby step at a time.

When a new business is started up, it has an obvious effect on the surrounding community. Being entrepreneurial in your life is no different, especially with the more important things. If we become proactive thinkers, then we will solve problems in life before they become crises. Proactive behavior means acting on the environment around you long before it has time to react on you. It can turn a gaping injury into a tiny scratch, or a small favor into an epic force of servitude.

Think about the people who started the social organization *Invisible Children*. This is a non-profit group that is trying to put a stop to the social genocide and militarization of young children in Uganda, Africa. In 2003, three young filmmakers went to Africa on a random filmmaking adventure. They ended up stumbling upon Africa's longest-running war, which happened to be abusing and exploiting the use of young children in violent warfare. Here at this crucial moment is the definition of being proactive.

These three filmmakers could have turned around and told themselves that this war was not their issue and that they had no say in such a huge conflict. Fortunately for millions, this is not what said. They began shooting footage of the war, and turned it into a revolutionary documentary. This film was able to help found the organization and start raising millions of dollars to alter these horrible tragedies. Nine years later they have mobilized a social army, raised millions of dollars, and are now standing a chance at ending the entire war. That is what I call making an impact.

Do they consider themselves entrepreneurs? Probably not. But they acted entrepreneurially, and showed the rest of the world that they could change the tides of war with a camera, compassion, and years of tenacity. When they stumbled upon this atrocious situation in Africa they instantly acted, and were proactive in their cause. They saw the opportunity to help these innocent people, especially these children used as pawns in a horrendous war. Their value proposition, to save countless lives with their video cameras and their cause, was tenaciously carried out. This documentary was then combined with the relentless force of everyone else that helped found *Invisible Children*, and has succeeded in driving this remarkable social mission.

This whole movement and idea started as a pebble dropped in the ocean. Now look at the tidal waves the initial ripples are creating. The benefits of acting entrepreneurial can be exponential and world-changing. The various and inspirational effects from the *Invisible Children* started by these three young men has now been felt by several nations and countless people all over the world. I would encourage visiting their website (www.invisiblechildren. com) and taking a look at their cause. It is fascinating, inspiring, and uplifting. I do what I can to donate to organizations like this; organizations that I believe in. It may not be much, but I decided to be a little entrepreneurial about their cause as well.

In addition to donating money from time to time, I bought a shirt from them and decided to help the cause out a little in my everyday life. I make an effort to make sure the shirt is worn at least once a week, all day, so that I wear it frequently. Because people always ask what the shirt means, I am now able to spread the word about the *Invisible Children* cause, and help out in my own individual way. Like I said, it may not be much, but it's an additional way to make an impact.

> "Do just once what others say you can't do, and you will
> never pay attention to their limitations again."
> —James Cook

This next example may seem silly and trivial, but the results speak for themselves. In our classes they tell us to be entrepreneurial about anything, and trying new things always pushes room for potential benefit. I realized while in class one day that the standard line-by-line method by which I took notes was very boring to me.

These notes were difficult to study afterwards because everything was so boringly listed and written out. A small entrepreneurial idea drifted into my head, and I decided to be proactive and act on my idea; I figured I would give it a shot.

Note-taking became an exercise to not only soak in the information in class, but to write and jot things down in a creative and out-of-the-ordinary fashion. I would write things in bubbles, write giant headings and then have the sub points flying around the corresponding titles, or write down key points in a humorous or sarcastic style. It may seem like that would be nothing but a distraction to note-taking, but it ended up helping me out a lot. Reading my notes is not as laborious as it used to be, and it is always kind of fun to think of new things to do as I am jotting things down. If it creates value, then it is worthy of sticking around.

A large portion of being entrepreneurial is living proactively, but in order to move in this direction we have to be very observant of our exterior environment like a sponge that soaks in everything. I have heard this kind of mentality described as "pulling the tooth." If there is an issue in your life, do not let the tooth sit there and rot. Pull the problem out, and relief yourself of the pulsating pain. There are many situations that could call for such responses, such as an argument with a friend. Be the first to take a step forward and offer a conversation. If any two people are to be friends again, someone will have to take the first bow.

I can be stubborn in these situations, and it always makes me feel guilty afterwards. When we are talking about two friends being in an argument, I think of it as wasted time. We can all get more money, but time is something you can never get more of. Every second is being spent, whether you are happy with how you are spending it or not. The more good times we pass up because we are stubborn and have an unwillingness to approach the other person first, the more life slips through our fingers. Being proactive can do more than just catch a good opportunity by its tale; it just might turn your life around.

I was once in an odd phase with my best friend, Nick, for a little while. I had become frustrated with him for various reasons, including our filmmaking and our social lives, and stubbornly did not want to be the one to approach him first. Eventually, he approached me and asked me what the deal was. He may not have agreed with my concerns, and he definitely may have not felt like he should be the one to extend a hand out for peace. But he did, and I have never forgotten that. He asked if we could meet up sometime soon because he wanted to talk with me. I agreed, and after we met and hashed everything out on the table, I could tell just how much he cared.

The difference in being entrepreneurial and just reacting to things as they happen to us is much like the relationship we have with cologne, perfume, or deodorant. Deodorant prevents the negative smells from occurring, but cologne and perfume puts a foot forward, and takes personal smell to the next level. This kind of mentality can completely change the way we interact with other people, and in turn, how they interact with us. Being entrepreneurial and proactive may do more than turn a life around; it could end up saving someone else's life. You never know.

The quicker we rid the negatives in life, the less pain is inflicted. Procrastinating those important moments in life that bring us happiness or closure does nothing but cost us happier times that could be better spent. I need to keep this in mind for future situations. From arguments with friends to projects I do not feel like doing, the quicker we pull that tooth the better. The dentist may take their sweet time, so take it upon yourself. That tooth will do nothing but spread infection if we leave it in there, and that will only cause it to hurt that much worse on the day we finally pull it.

You could even take this book as an entrepreneurial example. I am not writing this book for a class, nor am I writing it to make some amount of financial profit. I wanted a way to help others and offer myself out there to many individuals that could experience it at the same time. Next thing I knew, I was shoulder-deep in writing my first book and I was writing as much as I could. I wanted to create value for others and saw a niche for a book like this. All that was left was execution; and here it is.

"If you want to stand out, don't be different; be outstanding."

—Meredith West

Businesses ventures exist because of entrepreneurs. Change in the world comes from acting entrepreneurially. Recognize your opportunities, no matter how big or small. Whether it be a new way to spend your weekends or how to eat together as a family, opportunities come in all shapes and sizes. Keep your eyes peeled; those opportunities are everywhere. Combine your resources to do something about it and proactively fight to bring your value proposition to life. Anyone can sit in their room and think of good ideas all day. Acting entrepreneurially turns those thoughts and ideas into a reality; into a movement. Start your ad*venture* today.

CHALLENGE YOUR PERCEPTIONS

Your perceptions are how you interpret your world. The world you know and talk about is only communicated from one point of view: your own. Your explanation and schema of the place you call home is only that way because of how you see it. Perceptions affect you and how you feel because of your personal experiences and opinions that you bring to the table. That is just one perception. There are over six billion. I wonder which one is correct. Process of elimination? You would have to be joking.

Our values, opinions, perceptions, interpretations, and beliefs shape how we act, live, smile, share, love, and function. If you want to know who you are just ask yourself: *why do I think that? Why do I believe this way?* If you find yourself wandering in circles, we have a problem. You have become a dog chasing your tail and everyone is laughing and taking pictures.

For us to know exactly what it is we believe, how we got to that certain point, and why we have stayed there, we have to question ourselves. This is not suggesting that you go out and immerse yourself in the disagreed or even jump out into conflicting environments. It is, however, suggesting that a legitimate argument can never be made for something if you do not come prepared. We will all have days where our opinions are tested, and on that day I hope you already know the answers.

You may be asking, "Why does this matter? Who cares if I know every answer about my opinions? They are my beliefs, and that is that." Take an obviously related subject like religion. If you were asked today why you believed the way you did, would you know why? Would you be able to make sense when explaining it to someone else, especially someone who disagrees with you? If you are not able to emulate something to yourself, it will not come out to others very clearly either. In effect, the more you know about your own perceptions, the more you truly know yourself.

In addition to all of this, knowing our own perceptions helps us take off our jaded set of goggles. We all walk around with these goggles that contort the world around us to align with our own belief and judgment systems. Beer goggles are an interesting invention. They distort everything and tear up our vision clarity that would normally be unimpaired. Our own opinions are no different. So, if we are aware of why we believe what we do we start seeing our biases. We all have tilts in situations and preferences for things in life. The more aware we are about our own biases and "goggle drunkenness," the more we can try to keep things in line. We can begin to walk a little more carefully and lead with our hands, so that we avoid stumbling into a wall.

> "All our knowledge has its origins in our perceptions."
> —Leonardo da Vinci

For example, I know I am more likely to take quick offense to certain things and be overly sensitive because that is how I am emotionally strung. I see remarks a little differently than other people around me, and if I realize that I am being hyper-sensitive sometimes, then I can see what I am distorting and not get bent out of shape over nothing. It may have been a sarcastic joke or a tone that did not really mean what I inferred. Stopping and taking our goggles off can do more than prevent a trip or stumble. It might just end up straightening out the entire room.

A perception of mine that I have challenged a lot throughout my pendulum years of adolescence is my friendships, and how I should deal with them as time went on. In Owasso, it is not hard to find yourself hanging out with the same koi pond of friends from age six to sixteen. Owasso is a decent-sized suburban town with a graduating class consisting of six-hundred people. It seems like a town where knowing everyone would be impossible, but sometimes it can seem all too small.

I grew up an only child, and I always wanted a sibling or two. I spent a lot of time as a child next to my parents, but as kids get older things change. I never enjoyed being alone and when I discovered that friendships could help me deal with such a feeling, it became a lifestyle. Throughout my teenage years, I arguably saw my friends every single day. Whether it be having people over or going to someone's house, I usually saw at least one friend of mine each day. I have always been a very social person, and I always love to be around those I call my friends. In any child's life, the infamous day approaches that their friendships will all change as people leave home and fly from the nest.

As the time grew closer that I would be spreading my wings and taking flight out of Owasso, I was scared. I could not imagine a world without my same group of friends that I had been around forever; my beloved posse, *The Group*. I could not stand the thought of moving and leaving behind all of the people that I grew up with, and these people who had helped me through my toughest times. Some of these same people were guys that I met when I was seven, eight, and ten years old.

I also had those companions who I had known for several years, and had become very close with. I talked about my worries a lot with those friends and shared my boiling fears. It just seemed weird to not constantly be around those people whom I had seen more than my own parents for most of my teenage years. I found myself possibly too nostalgic about it all, and wondered if it would be different when the day actually came to leave home. I wondered if I was scaring myself from my own shadow.

> "What you see and hear depends a good deal on where you are standing; it also depends on what sort of person you are."
>
> —C.S. Lewis

I did not know how it would be to live in a new town. I did not know how to make brand new groups of friends. I had lived in the same house since I was three years old, went to the same school district my entire life, and instead of hanging out with various groups of people, I merged all of my friends together over the years into one giant amorphous band known to us as *The Group*. What would life be like without these people? What would it be like to live in a city where I did not have a best friend yet? How would the nights go when the only person I knew inside and out within my surroundings was myself?

I thought about the possibility that I was just thinking this way because it was the only thing that I knew. I had lived in the same town my whole life and had not seen much of the world. Perhaps this was a mindset that would go away as soon as I moved away. Maybe this was just part of leaving high school and moving on.

Just like when a tree is uprooted and falls over. That tree is trying so hard to move anywhere at any pace, but its roots are so deeply planted that it ends up going nowhere. It falls over on its side, still chained to the Earth. Then it has no other option but to sit there and wait. This made me think of something: if I thought this way forever, could it possibly keep me here in Owasso for the rest of my life? I knew I did not want that. I was hoping to transfer from this small pond, and maybe to a different and bigger lake.

When the time came to transfer colleges and move away from home to live on-campus at Oklahoma State University, I knew that this would be a decent test of what I had feared; I would get to see how I felt about moving away and distancing my close friendships first-hand. As I moved from Owasso to Stillwater, where OSU is located, I was leaving a lot of those friends behind, but some of the others were already there at OSU. I would have an opportunity to see if what I had contemplated was true.

> "No two people see the external world in exactly the same way. To every separate person a thing is what they think it is—in other words, not a thing, but a think."
> —Penelope Fitzgerald

Let us flash forward to my perception that I have now. I have challenged and put my perception on this subject to the test countless times, and that perception has changed a lot because of it. Since moving to OSU, the dynamic of those around me whom I call my close friends has changed vastly; more than I imagined could happen in a year's time.

Most of the people that I talk to every day are all people whom I did not even know a year ago. A lot of my closest friends that I used to see every day have now become people that I talk to every now and then, and see only a few times a year. It is such a striking feeling when I think back on it and realize how much it all has changed, but there is an important key element: it does not scare me anymore. I have begun to see that as life changes, so does our surroundings that spin about us for better or worse. In a tornado, grab your necessities and hunker down.

I have met more people since I arrived at OSU and I have had more social interactions in my time here than the entirety of my life beforehand. I have had time in my year and a half thus far at OSU to make handfuls of friendships. Some of them are still my best friends and some of them I do not talk with very much anymore. Life and the conversion of the people around me changes so rapidly, and it just took living around it to recognize its natural importance. The more it happens, the more I get used to it. It becomes a casual desensitization, if you will.

I strived to get very involved and plugged in once I got to OSU, and I strived to prove wrong both myself and my currently held perceptions. I tried to show myself that meeting and making new friends is not necessarily the same thing as destroying old friendships or burning bridges. It is just making lemonade out of the lemons that are handed to us. My older friends that I do not talk to every day are still just as good of friends to me. The logistics of my relationships with them are the only thing that is different. I can go weeks without talking to my best friend back home, but when I do see or talk with him, it is just another day back in high school. We are still the same two buds. The lemonade that you made before isn't thrown out. It is still in the fridge and is just waiting to be poured into a nice tall glass when you get the chance.

On the other side of the coin, as the time comes to move out of Oklahoma and transition to the Dallas, Texas area for my job after college, nostalgia steps into the ring with me. I am saddened every time I realize that the old hangouts will never come again. Our zany group of friends will never be the same as we once were. Countless memories come back to me now as I drive around Owasso, and I begin to feel as if I am in one of those notorious move scenes. Those transitional periods in a movie where the central character is remembering everything about a situation as they are out for a drive alone. Except there are no cameras or reminiscent music to help me deal with my thoughts. There are just the memories of what we all once shared and the perception that brings me the bravery to move on and replant such strong roots in another place.

Instead of being a fallen tree chained to the ground, or a ship whose travel is never anchored, my perception about friendships is like a school bus. As the bus travels its route and picks up new people, none are discarded. People are only picked up, not forgotten and left alone waiting on the street corner. I now know that our old friends will always be precious and dear to us. The bonds we make in life will stay special, but new ties are not to be feared. They are to be relished, because one day they will be just like the rest of the bonds. These pieces will all fall into place some day and build a puzzle; one that serves as our strong set of memories and relationships kept with love and adoration.

> "The voyage of discovery is not in seeking new landscapes but in having new eyes."
>
> —Marcel Proust

In a way, knowing that I believe this way has led to me being more comfortable with making these new transitions. It has let me be more confident as I run through the dark in life, arms outstretched. I clutch in the night for new friends and comforts as life twists and turns, not fearing the unknown. Sure there are bad things out there that could bite me, but the only way to know is to try for myself. If I did not reach or walk about, I would be just like that tree sitting there and waiting for spring to bring my leaves back. But you know, even those are only temporary.

I have always said that an idea never challenged is a car never crash tested. It is not safe, and it is anyone's guess what may happen if the stability or security of the idea is ever challenged and put to the test. We must not walk blindly about the world and just rattle off whatever our ears pick up. We have to take the blindfold off, walk our own path, and think for ourselves. When we form our own opinions and concepts for things in life, we must build them upon some sort of foundation. Please never be caught speechless when asked about why you believe in or why you do something. If you did not know why you believed in it, but were doing it anyway, I fear what else you might be capable of.

If I had not challenged my perceptions on developing and making new friends, I would still fear meeting new people and moving to new places. That blindfold is a lack of questioning and concern for where you stand on your issues, beliefs, morals, and other various viewpoints. The piñata dances around in front of us, and without that blindfold on, we know exactly where to hit and when. One hit and the candy is everywhere. Start untying that blindfold today.

CHASE YOUR PASSION

Being an entrepreneurship student, this may be the thing I hear the most frequently in my classes: our passion is what makes us and should be what drives us. Of course, they are also suggesting that we chase our passions in life, not just money, as we embark into our careers. We know how this country works, however.

Basically, in my own life, I have noticed that the number one thing that stirs about a good feeling and brings overall happiness to people is their passion. Before you even read this chapter, think about it: what are you passionate about? What gives you purpose in life?

We all have something that we are passionate about: cooking, football, family, music, traveling, art, dancing, baseball, cars, gymnastics, movies, video games, books, collections, and photography are just a few examples of things people may consider a passion of theirs. Once we have identified what we are passionate about there is nothing else left to do with that information than to exploit it. Passion can lead us to great amounts of intrinsic value, and if we are lucky, some extrinsic value as well. Those individuals who work in jobs they are absolutely passionate and crazy about have a great thing going for them, and I guarantee it shows in their lives and spirits. They have the life.

You may be asking yourself: *if my passion is merely a hobby of mine and that is all I care for it to be, then what do I need to be chasing?* I merely believe that being as close and interactive with your passion as you can is an amazing thing to try and do for yourself. I have talked with many others about their passions, aspirations, and other involvements they wish to fulfill in the future. The things people become passionate about are ultimately what they begin to live for and enjoy the most as time goes on.

A friend of mine recently confessed feeling useless and she felt like she did not stand for much. She said there was a lull in her life and it frustrated her. It was summer, and she thought she should be feeling on top of the world. We talked things over and she ended up finding some stored-away passions of hers, knew how she could chase these things, and felt a lot better. She loved running, baking, and she also renewed her excitement for her major. She started new goals for running long distances and was going to get involved in benefit run events in the Tulsa area. There was an online community for creative baking, and she had decided she may join that. That wonderful smile of hers was beginning to make a comeback. Sometimes, our passions give our turbulent world a little solidity. Seems a worthy pursuit, does it not?

I hope that everyone will have the chance to first find their passion and then chase it throughout life. Usually when we chase something and catch it, we are done with it. When then, do we *catch our passion*? When children in rural areas chase lightning bugs in the summer just to watch them glow within the palms of their hands, is it all over after that? No. The bug is let go, and the wonder and adoration continues until yet another lighting bug is within their grasp. We are no different, you and I.

I currently have several petty passions in my life. Some may be considered silly, but they are things that I truly enjoy. Some are more serious types of passion. From singing along with my favorite music which always makes me feel at ease, to watching my favorite movie, *The Dark Knight*, on a regular basis, there are plenty of things I enjoy. I love making short films with friends, talking philosophy and psychology with others, and trying out new things. Some of our passions are smaller and no less important to our enjoyment and ultimate fulfillment in our lives, but they cannot really be chased.

However, we can live these smaller passions and exploit them as often as possible. To *chase* a passion is to harness it to its full potential, and for the sake of relating it to my own personal story, to fulfill it as a career. Do you have a passion you could turn into a career? Would you ever dare to?

> "If your dreams do not scare you, they are not big enough."
>
> —Ellen Johnson Sirleaf

To make a living off of a passion of mine is my ultimate goal, not picking my career based on how much money it will make me. It means a lot to me to be able to see others benefit from something that I created, or that I built from the ground up. One way of making a living from doing such a thing is starting and owning an *actual* business of my own that helps other people.

This all started off where most stories like this one start: as a little kid. As a young six-or-seven-year-old boy, I dreamed of owning my own veterinarian clinic. I wanted to own my own clinic so I could personally help animals and be the one responsible for nursing them back to health. I may have hated needles or the thought of blood, but that was negligent when it came to helping out cute little animals. They needed care, and someone to hold them on their tougher days. That desire occurred early and had stuck ever since, until my earlier years as a teenager.

Somewhere around the age of thirteen I decided in a happenstance sort of way that I wanted to become an accountant. My mom always encouraged me to pursue something involving numbers since she thought I was so talented at math. I did not know anything about any careers, so I picked an accountant because I had two family members who were Certified Public Accountants. Heck, they lived comfortably, and they enjoyed their jobs. Ultimately, I decided to jump on their bandwagon and start my path towards being a CPA.

That flame died out in less than two years. My then-long-term girlfriend's mom was an accountant and I had been asking her a lot of questions every now and then. I knew I would be able to do the job in the future, but I started wondering if that is what I truly wanted. The itch for something that I would never get tired of started to turn me restless. A career path that just teased me with excitement and eagerness is what I really wanted. Thinking about being an accountant did not really do that for me, believe it or not. Even at sixteen years old.

I started getting the notion about that time that maybe I wanted to own my own business. Being my own boss, pursuing my own ideas, and building something from the ground up would be something I would love to be able to do. I had no idea what kind of business, where, or how. But I knew that maybe this is what I would do some day. Rogers State University was my first, tiny baby step.

While at RSU, I started two different non-profit car clubs in my hometown with people who shared my interests: customizing our cars and helping others out. During this time, a small-time film production organization by the name of *German Turkey Productions* was also birthed, founded by my friend Nick (the editor of this book) and me, which supported our independent filmmaking. We made a website, produced short and feature-length films, and shared countless memories in those days. All three organizations have faded over time since their inception for various reasons but one thing remains the same about them: they were an exercise of my spirit to cultivate new things.

In my time at OSU inside the Entrepreneurship curriculum, I have done many different things that align with my passion. From business models and business pans to critiques and competitions, there have been so many ways I have been able to put my passion to work, and ultimately, to test. I have started realizing in these classes that this was not only something that I could definitely see myself doing with my career, but something I would absolutely love to be able to do, period.

> "The more intensely we feel about an idea or a goal, the more assuredly the idea, buried deep in our subconscious, will direct us along the path to its fulfillment."
> —Earl Nightingale

While at OSU, I have founded an organization on campus for students like me who enjoyed being involved in film, by the name of the *Oklahoma State University Film Makers Association*. Following the process outlined in *Be Entrepreneurial*, I decided to start up the organization. It was a tedious and laborious process, but one I am so glad that I stuck with and completed. The club may not be very big, or anything special, but it is meaningful to me and some of its members. That is what it is all about.

As time went on, my perceptions were changing, and my aspirations to start a business took a more refined direction. Through influences from my role in Residential Life as a Resident Assistant at OSU, some of my classes, and many of the books I have read over the past few years, I came to a decision; I wanted to be a social entrepreneur. I did not want to work for a corporation that just fed money to higher-ups and helped make their pockets thicker. I wanted to own a business (or do something else) that helps other people, plain and simple.

I have found that my passion derives from making a difference in the world I live in, and starting a business is just one of those possibilities. I want to benefit those in need, and help those people who need it most. There are so many businesses evolving and starting up today that have other people in mind. I want to show my humanity and my love for those who are in need. Making a difference in this world is a passion of mine, and one I plan to chase down and secure for myself as a career.

A few months after I started thinking about a socially-driven career, I got an odd email asking me if I would like an interview. The company's name was *Teach for America*, and I had never heard of it before. I was very unsure of the legitimacy of this email, but once I started doing research, I realized something: this would be a perfect way to fulfill my passion right out of college. Getting to help close the education gap by teaching in at-risk and inner-city schools sounded like something I would love the chance to do. I replied back, went through several levels of interviews, and now I will be teaching in the Dallas-Ft. Worth area after I graduate from OSU.

The program lasts a minimum of two years, and then people are allowed to either stay or pursue other employment opportunities. As the time gets closer for me to step into the classroom, I am beginning to have a feeling. I have started to wonder if, after experiencing teaching with these kids during my first year, I will end up sticking with this for the rest of my life. I will get to have such an impact, help countless students out who really are in need, and I would get to make a career out of something invaluable: my passion. Regardless of how long I end up staying with the program, one thing is for sure: I am so excited to start having an impact, and make a difference in the world. That is the kind of career I am looking forward to.

All of these examples over time speak about one thing: I have been chasing what I could of my passion. These may all be little baby steps, but these steps are exercising my drive and harvesting the possibilities that arise out of doing so. That certain pursuit is different for everyone, so we should all try to be understanding when hearing from others about their own unique journey in pursuing their passions. I, personally, do not want to live an average life. I want to change the world one life at a time. I want to do something that matters to more than just me or my bank account.

> "Passion and purpose go hand in hand. When you discover your purpose, you will normally find it's something you're tremendously passionate about."
>
> —Steve Pavlina

I encourage you to think about yourself and what you could wake up every morning and do for a living and truly enjoy it each day. Imagine not dreading going to work . . . ever. Think about being excited to be able to get back to the pavement each week. None of us dream, as kids, of living the eight-to-five life where we dread the work week, and only live for the weekends. Somehow, many of us end up doing just that. Instead of falling into such a trap, I encourage finding that passion of yours and chasing it, while also keeping in mind the theme from *Keep Tenacity*. Do not sit and watch your passion spin about you. Reach out and grab it. And grip it ever so tightly.

I, like most, have had a job that I hated. I have worked for companies I did not like. Most of us have had work weeks that seemed to siphon from the very existence of our youth. It drains us, and it is nowhere near an exciting feeling. Our careers and jobs will take up about one-third of our lives, and they will encompass almost half of our time spent awake. Do you wish to dread and hate half of your entire waking life?

A friend of mine has shared a certain conversation with me several times about this very same thing. His name is Jordan, and he is in a college major that he does not really take any pride or joy from, but sticks to it for a few reasons. His college is getting funded by his parents, who happen to repeatedly insist that he stay in the major he is currently in because they say that it will make him good money someday. They feel that getting a job and making solid paychecks is the bottom line to his career, period, regardless of how happy it truly makes him. In addition to this, the exact major he would pick, if he were to switch, is uncertain. His dreams are fuzzy. There is one thing he knows for sure: he loves being creative, and wants a career where he can let his mind loose.

Jordan has a knack for making song parodies, and is so good at coming up with new and creative ideas. Who knows the possibilities if he were to jump out there and give something crazy a shot? Owning some creative business, writing songs for someone, making music videos or short films, or maybe even a screenwriter. A passion is trying to take flight here, it just needs its wings, and then it will be free. Jordan, like so many others, has the yearning to fly from the safety of the nest for the bigger possibilities in the sky. He just needs some crosswinds under his wings. What about you?

We only get one crack at this weird thing called life. Why do some of us seem to be so complacent with feeling like we have wasted it? You do not want to live with regrets that haunt you each night as you lay down to sleep. You do not want to look back at your life and wish you had done everything differently. Instead, when we looked behind us in life, it would be nice to have a garden of memories that bring us our own unique feeling of joy. So spend your waking life wisely, just like that money in your pocket.

Many people would defend themselves and say that they cannot afford to quit their jobs and just do what they want. People may say they do not have a passion that can be turned into an eight-to-five job. If we throw in the towel in a breathless sentence, we are just giving up and sacrificing the rest of our time here. Would you fight for the ones you love? Then why not fight for yourself? Find that passion of yours, chase it, and do not give up on it. Live what you love. Always.

If you lost a twenty-dollar-bill in a windy parking lot, would you just stand and watch it skip away? I would not just be standing there, I know that. I would chase down that dollar bill and secure it tightly back in my pocket. That is twenty dollars. The objects and pursuits in life that bring us passion are so much more important to us than some twenty dollar bill, even if we do not cognitively think about it too frequently. Our passion is extremely valuable and it is something I deem incredibly worthy of chasing down and claiming for ourselves.

Your career is calling. How are you going to answer the phone this time?

HOLD THE DIAMONDS OF OTHERS

You have people in your life that you see every day. But for whatever reason, they are no more than an acquaintance. You have those you know well, and that you may even consider a friend. Then, you have your best friends, those who you can always count on. The positive qualities that we love about our best friends and closest family members are easy to recall. The diamonds in their character seem to naturally present themselves. Sometimes, however, the tides can change, and do so very quickly.

Originally, I had an entirely different Pillar in mind for this section of the book. Those plans changed, however. The themes of this new Pillar ring truer than those of the Pillar that I had originally intended to insert here. This new theme was born out of a considerably intense situation that occurred between me and a long-time close friend of mine, who gave me permission to use his name in this book, named Steven, in early July of 2011. I was taught a valuable life lesson in a very close-to-home sort of way.

The original Pillar was *Surround Yourself With What You Wish to Become*. The idea centered on the progression of our social lives and who we choose to surround ourselves with as we grow older. The pillar insinuated that we should befriend and hang around the kind of people that we want to emulate, to make friends with those we respect and admire. The theme also implied dropping or fading away from those who did the opposite: people who were nothing near what you aspired to be like, and those who could even distract you from what you aspired to become. That Pillar tracked my progression along such thoughts, until a certain situation gave rise to a new idea. That new idea is this Pillar.

> "Appreciation is a wonderful thing: it makes what is excellent in others belong to us as well."
> —Voltaire

I have a lot of trouble practicing what I write in this Pillar. It is probably something that many others also have trouble with, which is exactly why I felt strongly to include this Pillar in the book. I tend to take a negative characteristic or two about someone and let it corrupt my whole perception of that individual. I can become too nit-picky over the flaws of another person, which tends to breed frustration and hostility toward them, and they do not deserve that. It is something I need to work on. I should flip the coin over and look at the other side. I believe the diamonds of a person's character—their good qualities that make them special—to be much more valuable to point out. We must strive to see the good and wonderful in others, and in a lateral way, appreciate them.

This story has its humble beginnings back in the ages of Owasso Mid-High, when Steven and I started becoming friends. We met each other through mutual friends and started hanging out together after school when we were fourteen years old. Back then, all we cared about were video games and the day when we would be able to get our driver's permit. We did everything together and became close friends pretty quickly, sharing plenty of hilarious, frustrating, and odd experiences. Our friendship matured over the years, and our ties ran deeper with time.

Both of us went through high school as very close friends and waded upstream through a lot together. From interactions with police officers, up and down girl situations, a car wreck, vacations, transitioning to different colleges, and countless other memories, we have bonded together a history book full of stories and memories, both good and bad. Over time, we both experienced many things in life and developed our own tracks to race through as we grew up.

I would not say we necessarily drifted as friends, but our friendship itself altered and morphed alongside our different personalities.

Steven and I had our inside jokes. There were the nights that we stayed up and ranted about everything that we hated. We both taught ourselves to shoot and edit film at the same time, and we both loved to make short comedic films back in the day. We both fixed and worked on our first cars, and we always had stories to tell others. A story we always reminisce about is when Steven got his first moving violation ticket. It was one of the first days out in his 1970 Camaro after getting his license, and we had just left my house. He sped up pretty fast after a stop sign, showing me the exhaust and the speed of the car. The next thing we noticed was not the sound of the exhaust, but instead a police officer at Steven's window handing him a ticket. Of all the situations he could have been in, that officer was there at just the right time and place. When any big news would occur in our lives, we would be the first to tell each other. Story after story, from laughter to tears, when we get on a tangent about our memories in high school, it lasts all evening.

After high school, our relationship became centered on certain timely events because we ended up at two different colleges. Steven and I only talked on the phone occasionally and saw each other on certain weekends or breaks from school. We stopped living life right next to each other, sharing our stories as they happened, and transitioned into sharing stories with each other in order to catch up. We had our own lives, friends, and stories to share now. The entire dynamic of everything around us changed. Change happens with time, and it is something that happens to every friendship. It just depends on how we all handle the changes that are swept our way.

Steven and I both have strong personalities, and our big group of friends that we had throughout high school was made up of about twelve different people. One could say that Steven and I were, in some metaphorical and weird way, the two parents, or leaders, of some weird and zany family. Both of us often hosted events, gave advice and some subtle sense of leadership, and often brought new people into our group of friends that we all coined as "The Group."

As you can see, our friendship had become much more than just Steven and me since those first days. It involved a lot of people, time, and relationships. It was more than just feelings that were affected on the night this Pillar refers to. It was an entire life story.

This Pillar-defining event occurred one evening while at a get-together hosted by a mutual friend. We were catching up with each other—having not seen each other in awhile because of the different roads college was driving us down—and we somehow got to the topic of the current state of our long-tenured friendship.

A few questions stirred some conversation about how I was frustrated with our friendship as of late. He ended up asking me what it was about him that had been bothering me; he wanted to know why we weren't as close as we once had been. Steven and I had been best friends for many years throughout our youth, but over the past couple of years, we had slowly been drifting apart. I had a problem with holding onto the diamonds that made Steven unique, and I was frustrated. Before I started speaking, I did not take the time to consider many things, including his feelings. I told him several of my thoughts, and the results were not pretty.

> "The friend is the man who knows all about you, and still likes you."
>
> —Elbert Hubbard

I told Steven that I did not think he had the characteristics of someone I aspired to be more like, a quality that I found was increasingly important for me to find in friendships. He was also told that I did not see him being a friend of mine in five years because of these looming doubts, and that I had doubted our friendship for some time now. I continued by saying that I did not see him express passion in life that often, that I felt like he was somewhat selfish in the way he acted, and I mentioned some other things I ended up regretting having said. He got upset and reacted with anger. He was at a loss for words. Though I tried so hard to explain my thoughts, I was horrible with my wording and expression of what I was feeling.

I had said things that could be considered heinous to a friend I'd had since I was fourteen years old. This had gone very wrong.

When two kids are fourteen years old and consumed in nothing but TV shows and little jokes, a serious conversation or issues of compassion and trust do not tend to come up too often. When these two kids begin to grow up, evolving to manhood, and enter their senior years of college, life tends to resonate a little differently from the airs of conversation. We started having more serious conversations more frequently, and we seemed to start caring about different things. Steven and I had grown up in each others' presence, and as expected, we had different paths along the way. We had both grown up in our own ways, and parts of us were just as fourteen-years-old as ever. In essence, we viewed maturity and held the definitions of what close friends should be differently and acted accordingly because of it. That disconnect is what was careening this situation off a cliff and is what wrecks many other damaged relationships and friendships today.

He was very hurt, and with good reason. What had I said to him? I felt awful and later regretted everything that came out of my mouth during our discussion. He said a few things in his defense that stuck to me like persistent leeches. He told me he would not trade his childhood for anything-that same childhood that I was a major part of, with those years full of stories and memories that we shared. He told me that the friends we disagree with in life strengthen us, and challenge us to grow. And most importantly, he mentioned the gems, or diamonds, in others' lives. He mentioned how we can find good in our friends, which should be what we hold on to, not the negatives. And you know what? I agree.

We did not speak to one another for a little while. Many complicated situations followed these events. Mutual friends of ours heard what had happened and wondered what I had been thinking or saying about them. This whole group of friends, our own sort of "family" that the two of us seemed to harbor, was concerned and confused. A few were angered, several were worried, and some were just confused by the two sides of the story. I felt like Steven had overreacted in his descriptions of the event with other people after the altercation, but who knows how I would have reacted if I was suddenly faced with this kind of situation? He felt betrayed, and I could understand that. I had said a few hard-to-swallow statements to a long-time friend of mine, someone I had shared memories and laughs with for over six years.

What usually happens with arguments between two people, especially close friends, is that the argument ends up affecting those surrounding the two people. Our situation was no different. Our group of friends—"the group"—had seen and been through so much together that we were all practically family and this definitely shook the dinner table. Other people heard about what was happening and were filled with anxious questions. This did not help my frustration with how things had diverged from the original path, but I did start to realize how much damage I had initially started by my hurtful, inconsiderate comments. Your words are powerful, whether you mean them to be or not.

During these few days, countless thoughts ran through my head. So many emotions were waging war with each other that I feared my brain would just refuse to keep processing the situation anymore. There was a certain situation—one that occurred long before the incident that defines this Pillar—that I randomly recalled in those few days. There was a night Steven called me, and as I answered the phone, I heard him struggle to speak in a way that I had never heard from him before. He told me he was coming over, no question about it. Phone calls like these at three o'clock in the morning are usually not just another call to chat. I said "okay," and I waited for him to get to my place.

When I heard him approach my front door I stepped outside and I saw him making a face that I am still not able to get out of my head. That was a face of a man who literally did not know what to think next. He ended up telling me about how he had just found out that his girlfriend had been cheating on him. This was not just some one occasion incident either. She had been bragging about it via text messages and was repeatedly cheating on him with another guy. I had never heard or seen him cry, or talk in that tone of voice, and I had never had a conversation like that with him.

Conversations and nights like those are things I will never forget, no matter what happens on down the road from here. Thoughts like that brought me right back to those critical moments, and I knew he was my good friend. We just needed to speak again.

When we did speak again, our conversations were coated with awkwardness. Neither of us wanted to be the first to apologize and admit that we had been in the wrong. We talked about every little aspect of the situation so that both of us could try to think it through and grasp many of the loose ends. I ended up confessing to him that I was sorry for what I had said, how I presented myself that night, and how I had acted. He apologized for how he reacted afterward and for the events that happened as a result. I realized that I had not been very appreciative or grateful as of late, and he knew that he had taken the situation a little too far. Things were beginning to get glued back together.

We both had a lot of thoughts flying around in our heads in relation to this event, and we both felt that what we had done had both good and bad parts. The one thing that we could agree on was that this kind of fight and argument was not necessary, no matter what level of friends we had somehow become. We knew that we were upset by the other person and the argument's effects on other people, but we needed to patch this up together. For two people to move forward, they need to be side by side, not in one another's faces. That mutual understanding helped close the disjunction, allowing the pieces to start falling back into place.

The respect that we had for each other and the desire not to let the friendship fall apart is what brought us back together. We were both willing to try and patch this up and to put our heads together on such a sensitive and touchy situation. Hanging out again for the first time felt like I was with a brand new person, but we saw it in each other that we cared and that forgiveness was present.

"As we express our gratitude, we must never forget that the highest appreciation is not to utter words, but to live by them."

—John F. Kennedy

Since then, we are on brotherly terms again. I have a new view on things, including our friendship from here on out. He reminded me of a perspective that I had completely overlooked, something I should have already been doing. I appreciate the good he does in life, the gems he mentioned; the diamonds of his personality.

This experience with one of my best friends taught me a lot. Hopefully, you are able to relate to this experience in some way. Let us try not to let one instance of negativity, doubt, or anger ruin a personal relationship. If anything is to be generalized or remembered better than other things, it should be the good in other human beings. The splendid things in others, the diamonds, may be harder to find in some than others, but we all know why we have the friends we do. If we allow for frustration to spread and infect our mentality towards someone close to us, it can damage and injure in ways we may not have ever imagined. I saw it for myself, and that is how I was taught this Pillar; the hard way.

Having said all of this, we do not have to overlook everything that another person does to us. We choose our friends in life, and we all have to maintain our own perceptions of what is too much to disregard. That will be up to each and every one of us to decide in our own lives, when and if that time comes around.

We all have a different view on the friends that we hold onto, and our reasoning behind each and every decision we make that coincides with that. We can advance towards those we admire and aspire to be like, but shall we not forget those who helped make us who we are today? Our roots should never be forgotten, and we should always remember those in life that made us who we are today; each and every one of them. If it were not for them, you would not be who you are today, no matter the significance.

I had overlooked the facts about someone who had made up part of my roots, and I was letting my current frustrations poison my appreciation for someone that helped me grow into who I am today. I have Steven to thank for this Pillar, and for giving me a sort of wakeup call that changed a perspective of mine on life. Is there someone out there who used to be in your life that you split from in the past over something that seems so silly now? Is there someone who helped bring you to where you are today, who deserves a little more appreciation? It is never too late to make things right. Trust me.

Keep Tenacity

We have all felt like giving up. We have all battled a monster in life or scaled the face of a mountain; metaphorically speaking. Hundreds of stories could fill up a book telling us all about the glorious and marvelous ways that people overcame something, never gave up, and achieved something priceless for themselves. There could be numerous variations in these stories, varying amounts of success or hardship, and plenty of emotional appeals and testimonies, but one thing will remain true throughout. Preparing oneself for hardship is difficult to gift to someone; and impossible to wrap with paper.

Tenacity could be defined as the courage and will to motivate ourselves to keep pushing on through life no matter the conditions. It is an elusive concept. Even if we take a temporary spirit of confidence and tenacity away with us after reading stories and testimonies, it usually does not last for long. It will have to originate from nowhere, and you will have to pull it out from the middle of yourself; no matter the time or place. Unfortunately, eBay does not offer it on a *Buy it Now* basis.

Drive may be something we experience all by ourselves, but that does not mean that we cannot receive help along the way. The people and environments that surround us can foster or facilitate tenacity, but in the end, it is our very own responsibility. The sooner we can obtain the right mindset, the better. Some people say that we place more personal value on the things that we worked harder for. It is then safe to say that those same people would say that we would highly value anything that required hard work and perseverance to obtain. We have to keep on keeping on.

"Good luck is another name for tenacity of purpose."
—Ralph Waldo Emerson

For each one of us to hold tenacity, we first have to conjure it within ourselves. We have to derive the pure drive and brutal mentality of never giving up that lays dormant inside us. This can be hard, but on the same flip of the coin, it comes easier for others. For me, it happened over time as I leapt across each stepping stone in life and saw what perseverance and my own personal drive led me to achieve.

After coming to OSU and enrolling in the Entrepreneurship program, the word tenacity became common conversation topic. Every professor in the program attempts to engrain the behavior into our minds and lets us know it will be a vital ingredient in our success in the field of Entrepreneurship. But as you may have guessed, I was not always so familiar with the concept.

As a young man I began to play the piano around age seven. The piano may look easy to some, but it can actually be pretty challenging to learn, especially for someone like myself who is not overflowing with musical talent. I took piano lessons from a family friend throughout elementary school and played a few recitals here and there. My parents were very proud of their little piano player. Unfortunately, I was not very gifted with drive and commitment to the idea.

Practice makes perfect, but I must not have had my sights anywhere near that. Practice was utter torture for me, and I hated having to sit down and try to become better at playing the piano. Regular piano practice hours began to be enforced around our house and it became a chore for me very quickly. I was not learning as fast as I wanted to be, and I did not have the patience or the drive to make myself keep going. I dropped the piano-playing altogether around the age of twelve, making certain that piano practice would be completely ridden from my weekly agenda.

As I look back on it now I really wish I had stayed with it. My friend Isaac, who is a very skilled piano player, began with the same story that I did. He, unlike me, stuck with it and kept at it over the years. It has paid off, and he is now able to write and play his very own beautiful set of music. Every time I sit and hear him play, I wish that I would be able to sit down at such an instrument and have it make such a wonderful sound. Tenacity would have given me that opportunity.

I yearn to begin playing the piano again someday soon, and when I do so, I will be sure to stick with it this time. I love hearing the piano in person, and I would adore being able to play songs for both myself and others. My mom used to love to sit and listen to me as I played. I want to be able to give both of us that joy again; the enjoyment associated with me playing the piano.

Years later, after getting into making short films with friends of mine after school, tenacity and I got to have round two. This time it dealt with filmmaking. As I have mentioned in other parts of this book, I have been making short and feature-length films for years. I have gained experience and skill with every video, but there have been many times that I grew frustrated with a project I was working on. I taught myself all the styles and tricks that I currently use to write, film, produce, and edit videos. And I can say with certainty that this did not happen overnight.

One of the most challenging things about independent filmmaking is the budget that you are able to work with. I am currently in college and came from a lower-income family. This has led to very limited resources for me to be able to utilize. I do not know if I have ever paid anyone cash for having helped me with a project. I have taken people out to dinner, or bought them things in return for them sacrificing their time in order to help me, but it has never been a large amount of monetary compensation. I never had the money to get any professional lighting, audio, stage equipment, cameras or top-of-the-line editing software. I did what I could with what I had: two HD Sony Handycams, Sony Vegas 9 editing software, and the people around me. I have relied on the generosity and selfless service of many of my friends and people around me to complete some of the videos I have been involved in; and for that I thank them.

With that being said, in my years of filmmaking, I have certainly felt like throwing in the towel. There have been countless times when I have sat there after a filming session and felt like the video we were working on was nothing but a hopeless waste of our time. When I would not give up on those projects and when I would persist until the film was completed, it was such a rewarding feeling. This was especially the case when I completed each of the three feature-length films I created alongside my friend Nick (the editor of this book). There is not a feeling to describe finishing a feature-length film like that. Each film took months to complete, and involved many stressful evenings. But after it was all said and done, it was all incredibly worth it. Persistence paves the way so that you may harvest your own possibilities.

> "Confidence is not a guarantee of success, but a pattern
> of thinking that will improve your likelihood of success,
> a tenacious search for ways to make things work."
> —John Eliot

In those days, Nick and I would go to school or class, go to work, and then come together to film at night. That was what our days were like nearly every day. On many of those evenings, we were tired and would rather have been relaxing and unwinding than working hard on projects that may or may not get us anywhere. At times, it simply took away our youthful spirit. We took it very seriously and it drained so much of our time and effort. We could not have done it without our friends, of course; they were simply helping us out because we needed them, and it was greatly humbling and appreciated.

With the amount of work required to complete our films, we eventually burnt out many of those friends, and many of them become reluctant to help us film anymore. There were times when we would attempt to have people whom we did not know help us out, often referred by a friend or even people from Rogers States' drama department. The reality was that no one would want to volunteer their free time and not get paid for acting in a film for someone they did not know. I accepted the fact and I did not ever expect anything more. It was still saddening and frustrating though. When we were not filming on weekday evenings, we were sacrificing our precious weekend time to help each other make films. Sometimes the only motivation for Nick and me to keep going came from each other.

At that time, we were always trying to get noticed for co-making these films. We helped each other stay tenacious and continue working on it, no matter how ridiculous it sometimes seemed. As time went on and we completed more videos together we realized how much we liked completing each video. We knew the intrinsic value we achieved every time we got to see our projects displayed for our friends or on YouTube, even if the film may not ever go past that. The stone picked up speed as it furthered down the hill.

The resolve we experienced and accumulated over time really urged us along in our filmmaking. Without it, we would have given up on those cold winter nights when we ended up filming outside for seemingly-long hours at a time. Without tenacity, we would have stopped making videos when our first feature length film got ridiculed and did not go anywhere; when we got made fun of by our peers. We sold about 75 copies of that first film to friends and acquaintances, but that was about it.

The main point about the progression occurring in those days is that we grew tenacity as time went on and as we made more films. The more fun we had the harder we worked. That is the true purpose of the whole mindset. Internal fulfillment is priceless.

There have also been times where I have cut my filmmaking passions all-together and decided that it would not get me anywhere. I had peaks and valleys about my own personal growth and success along the way. There would be periods of time where I was really focused on film and it was all I would think about, and I became so ambitious and optimistic about the future of my endeavors.

Then there were times when I would feel put out and feel like I would never get noticed in such a highly competitive industry like filmmaking. There were other times I put filmmaking on the back-burner and I did not think about it too much. These apathetic times bred doubt about my future in filmmaking, and I tended to get a little depressed about the actual progress I had made over the years. I had put many videos on YouTube, made commercials, founded a filmmaking club at OSU, and showed so many people my work. But I never gave up hope.

I do not think you will sit there after reading this brief story in awe of my tenacity, mouth agape. I would not want that to happen either. As said before, I am simply sharing a part of my life with you to show you how I have proven the message of this Pillar to myself. My unwillingness to give up has helped me in countless ways. Now it is your turn. Think of a time when you never gave up and you ended up winning because of it. You achieved what you desired. Would you not want another story like that? How about twenty more?

"Learn to fail with pride, and do so fast and cleanly. Maximize trial and error by mastering the error part."
—Nassim Nicholas Taleb

With all of this said, I am not saying I am a master of persistent behavior by any means. I have so much to learn about holding this tenacity by its horns. I can get discouraged easily when a video of mine gets made fun of and mocked. I have the capability to be tenacious; I just need to learn to keep it pertinent. We should all keep that in mind the next time we trip a little. However, as they say, a stumble may prevent a fall. Tenacity may just be the helping hand that grabs us and allows for that. So keep holding; and hold on tightly. You are, after all, holding on for dear life.

LIVE FOR OTHERS

There is so much to be said about living for other people, because in all honesty, I find this to be the most important of all the Pillars. Arguably, this is the one Pillar that could support all of the others single-handedly. I have not always lived my life under the motto of *save the best for last*, but I felt it was appropriate for the structure of this book. The Primary-Recency Theory in psychology proposes that we will always remember the items at the beginning and end of a series better because of how our brain categorizes information. Therefore, I hope the ending will be one of the parts you will remember the most as you take what this book has to say with you in life.

Many people in history have stressed the importance of doing things for other people and the invaluable intrinsic rewards it provides. Numerous philosophers and people we herald as wise have said that living for more than ourselves is a good road to travel. In a crazy, cruel, and hectic world like the one we are born into, it can be difficult to continually put others before ourselves, or to completely take ourselves out of the equation.

We often stay wrapped up in looking out for our best interests as we attempt to grow and develop in the chaotic curve-ball environment the world throws us. There is so much that we all must look out for in our own lives, from our families to our health. Sometimes we can end up turning a blind eye to the rest of the world around us because of it and never think twice.

This Pillar and its message of living for others boils down to one thing: be selfless in our interactions and experiences with other individuals. Being selfless allows us to focus on servitude and dedication to other people and their own struggles. It allows our hearts to open up and grow exponentially, and it shows us how to benefit the rest of the world around us. Servitude makes a statement and takes a small step in the right direction; the direction needed to relieve some of the ugly burdens of this intense, pressuring world in the twenty-first century.

> "We are formed and molded by our thoughts. Those whose minds are shaped by selfless thoughts give joy when they speak or act. Joy follows them like a shadow that never leaves them."
>
> —Buddha

There is so much I want to say in regards to this Pillar; so much on my mind that I must try to put into words. I want to ramble on about how much it can affect the people around us, how easy it can truly be, and how much good it could do for the world we live in.

Remember the last time someone went out of their way to help you out? Maybe it was the time they went out of their way to pick you up from work, no matter how inconvenient it may have been for them. Or maybe it was the time they put your feelings before their own. Remember how that felt? The smile it put on your face? If we all took the time to be selfless and live for others, we could bring light to the darkness that often surrounds us; we could all light a candle and lead someone else through the night.

Living for other people, being selfless, living in servitude, or any other way you may put it sums up one sort of action: putting others before ourselves. This can seem foreign, illogical, and sometimes even unnecessary, but the more we do it, the more we see its wondrous secrets.

As humans, as animals, it is natural for us to sometimes only look out for ourselves and the things that matter to us. If everyone in the world followed this mindset, the world would fall apart in a matter of days. That's why we need those people to light their candles and keep the darkness from taking over. Those people in our lives that do so much for us, rain or shine, are the people cherished and appreciated the most in our lives. They are the ones we miss the most, the ones who make us smile. We often want to be like them, but what is it that often times keep us from doing so?

There is one example close to my heart, from my own personal experiences, that best illustrates the final theme of this book. A single person comes to mind. This is someone who has shaped my life for many years. She is someone I look up to, and I find the steps she takes through life to be increasingly selfless. Her heart is enormous in its potential, and she does so much for other people. Sometimes her mentality gets her walked on or hurt, but she tries to stay positive and continually do as much as she can to help those people in need around her. This wonderful person, whom I immensely adore and admire, is my own mother, Janet Snodgrass.

As my mother's son, I may be a little biased to herald my mom as one of the nicest and most sincere people I have ever known. I feel like she deserves so much in life, and I always wish she had more to enjoy for herself. She has gone through a lot, including many trying and hard times, but she perseveres. She has never had much money in life or owned many flashy things, but she was always overflowing with gratuity and love. If everyone lived with a heart like hers, the world would most definitely be smiling a lot more often.

One of the most recent things my mom has done is one act of service for which I am very proud of her. She joined an organization called Domestic Violence Intervention Services, or DVIS, and she is now a crisis responder for victims of rape and domestic abuse. She gets calls from a hospital in the area when a victim arrives, and she comes to help them fill out paper work as they ascend through their traumatic process. There is a lot to be done when someone who has been raped or abused is brought into the hospital, and my mom is an assistant and nurturer to aid, not only the victim in one of their most crucial and haunting times, but also to help the nurses on staff at the hospital as well. She has not made any money from any of it, never will, and she does not want to. What matters to her is the impact she has been able to have on others' lives. She was once a victim of a violent rape, and because of that she wants to help those hurt women out there going through complete and utter hell. I was so proud when she told me all of this, and I could not help but be so thankful that I could call someone as remarkable as her, my mommy.

Debt is something that infiltrates many lives in the twenty-first century. It has become a part of American life and something many people deal with every day. My mom has gone into additional debt, not for herself, but for the sake of her own father. It all started a few years ago when one of her brothers (we will call him Stan for clarity) attempted to gain sole power of attorney of my grandfather, to handle all of his finances and affairs on his behalf. This attempt for power came right after Stan had made allegations that my mom was partially at fault for the death of my grandmother, and their mother. This was not a simple or innocent legislative strife, and it would not end well for anybody.

Stan was reacting with anger, and the timing was curious, right after the death of their mother. It seemed like he was going to exploit my grandfather, who had Alzheimer's disease, and do God-knows-what in spite of the other seven siblings in the family. My mom, along with two of her sisters, stood against this injustice, and they challenged Stan in court. They both cared for their father a lot, even if he had not been the best father in the world to them while they were growing up. My mom stepped up to the plate and was ready to bat for an innocent human being.

At one point, my mom was ten-thousand dollars in debt from these legal battles alone. She was brave and determined to help her dad. The loan she had to take out was not for her next car, nor was it for some new wardrobe. My mom was defending her father and his finances from Stan and another sibling of hers who later joined in against my mom (we will call her Mary). There were eight siblings in the family, and the two who were conspiring were determined to do whatever it was they intended to accomplish. They could get away with it too, if they pulled all the legal strings while he was still alive. My mom was not going to have any of that, and she was going to stand up for the good in others around her, whether she had to do it alone or not.

My mom has endured so much pain and hurt because of the aforementioned situation, but she has tried to stay strong and keep fighting, no matter what it took. I have held her while she cried, when she felt like giving up. She felt helpless, scared about how this situation added onto our already looming debt and nervous about the never-ending court dates. My mom was tired of being yelled at and verbally attacked in and outside of the courtroom by people she grew up with. They even tried spreading nasty rumors about my mom throughout their family to try and get her to back down. Some of the things she has had to endure were hideous. This was no game.

The pure intentions and selfless strife of my mom's drive and commitment showed through, and she has won the legal battle for now. She may have felt like giving in, but she knew she could not give up on a fight she believed in as much as this one. She now gets to see my grandpa every day as he battles Alzheimer's, share a laugh with him, and she gets to know he is safe; even if his deteriorating mind does not always remember who she is or why she sometimes cries tears of joy when she is with him. She endured financial burdens, emotional grief, and much more just to protect her father in his last years. And you can bet she does not regret an ounce of it all. What would you go through for those around you?

I have witnessed other various situations when she has helped others; it seems to never end. She gave money for food, clothes, and rent to Mary-the same sister, who alongside Stan, sued my mom over my grandpa's situation. My mom even housed Stan years ago when he got out of jail and had no place to go. Once, she gave one of her sisters nearly two-thousand dollars so that she could move across the country and make ends meet. My mom's other brother got into a horrible life-altering motorcycle wreck, and since then, she has spent countless hours helping him rehabilitate and supporting his family through their darker days. She stayed selfless and respectful through it all, and she remained true to herself; true to what she believed in. I feel truly blessed to have grown up with a mother as giving as mine.

She has done countless things including taking sign language classes so she could sign sermons for deaf members at her church, keeping CPR certified so she could help someone in need, giving her coworkers money for food and Christmas gifts for their kids when they did not have enough money, and so much more. My mom also bought Christmas presents every year for my dad's own kids and grandkids from his first marriage, in spite of him saying that they did not need anything. She has always said that she will not let there be a child around her go through a Christmas without a gift to open. It does not matter if her money is tight or if she is stressed beyond belief from her demanding job. She keeps on giving and serving, and it literally goes on and on. Honestly, I just stand in awe.

> "Real love is when you become selfless and you are more concerned about your mate's or children's egos than your own. You're now a giver instead of a taker."
>
> —Sylvester Stallone

Throughout all these examples, one thing rings true. My mother, Janet, does not expect favors in return and she does not feel entitled to any sort of payback as her pile of servitude and favors accumulates. That becomes a very important part of acting for others; knowing that we do not earn or deserve anything back, just because we stuck our neck out there. My mom is just being herself, and she is just doing what she thinks is right and good for the world. It is so nice to see and be able to live around; it is truly inspiring.

I once saw a random, sourceless quote online that went something like this: "The sun has done so much for the Earth over millions of years, and yet, it does not ever ask for anything in return. If only we could all learn from the sun." That thought, and the said metaphor, has stuck with me ever since, and I think it is so true. I feel like this is what my mom is attempting to do for others. She is helping everyone, as much as she can, never expecting them to return her the favor, lend her money, or go out of their way for her. That unforgettable part of the whole process, taking ourselves out of the picture altogether, is what makes our acts of service truly selfless.

I feel like there is a certain *serve myself* mentality that many of us can get into, and often times, it will stick with us for the rest of our lives. I am no different; I am guilty of having this mentality for the majority of the financial aspects in my own life. Do you think the issues of the world are not worthy of your attention and time because it does not affect you? Or what is it that makes us not rise and act out for the well-being of others? I wish to change and be more selfless. I want to reach out and do so much for other people to end up having an impact like my mom does. Her radius of kindness is enormous, and is something I feel is worth applauding.

This *serve myself* mentality seems to bleed out every time I encounter a certain conversation I seem to have again and again with other people. I have put some thought into joining the Peace Corps after college, or a service like that, to help people in need. I want to help the lives of others, to live for more than just myself. When others hear about this certain idea, there is one response I hear a lot: "Why? That doesn't make you any money." What they probably do not consider is that I already knew that. I figured that out way before I put any thought into the idea.

I knew that I would only bring back about three thousand dollars a year for my service. The Peace Corps is considered a volunteer position. It is not for maximum profit, a new car, your next big house, or a new jet ski. It is for other people, not you. Why does something that defies acting only for ourselves seem so alien to many of us? Is it how we were raised, our country, our economy, or a fear of not being able to provide for ourselves, or our future families? Our efforts do not have to be directed at an organization like the Peace Corps. It could be a local act of service for lesser-privileged individuals that live right around us. It could be anything that spreads joy, instead of hoarding it for our own consumption.

If you could appreciate a helping hand from another soul in life, imagine how much these lesser-privileged individuals would love every bit of help and attention you gave them. We have such an amazing potential for change and for worldly progression; we just have to embrace the tools we already possess.

Here is just one simple example of the difference we can make: a woman from DVIS, the organization my mom joined, told us a story that had recently happened to her. She ran the clothing donation sector of DVIS, and a family came in that was practically homeless, with nothing to wear but what was already on their backs. A little girl, no older than six, ran up to the volunteer and hugged her leg as tightly as any six-year-old could. The volunteer looked down and noticed the little girl was crying. "Thank you," the little girl said. Not once, but over and over and over again. This little girl was wearing a used coat someone had donated. Most of us would scoff at the idea of wearing an old, used coat; however this little girl was sobbing with gratuity. You think you can't make a difference by helping others in even the smallest ways? Please, think again.

We all have our own opinions, but this is why I think many people around the globe hate the current image that gets painted of Americans. Many of them find us to be materialistic, partial to only ourselves, and simply self-serving. We get a cookie, or maybe even millions of them, and harbor it all for ourselves. As individuals, we will bite anyone who dares even look at what we have. From caring nothing about how much money we make, to consuming everything without ever considering the environment, there are a lot of criticisms for how we, as Americans, live our lives. Do not forget about how most popular songs that come out these days feature an artist that brags about how much money they have or how outstandingly cool they are. And we wonder why America gets a bad rap sometimes.

I am not saying that we should become homeless and give every single thing we own to someone else. I do think a progression in the selfless direction from where we are today would be a pertinent and good idea. This is not only in a sincere urge to save our country in this ever-evolving system of nations, or to make ourselves look better to those around us, but also to save humanity as it gasps for its last breaths.

"The best way to find yourself is to lose yourself in the service of others."

—Mohandas Gandhi

Living for others is something I hope to be able to do more of as time goes on. People say to give as freely as you take. We accept favors from other people pretty quickly. Should we not be even faster to deal them out? There are two situations that I personally encountered in my time here at OSU that I would like to share in regards to *Live for Others*. Each one is unique, but also appeals to this Pillar in their own way. In both cases, I tried to think of others before myself, and take myself out of the equation.

I was walking to class one day, listening to my iPod as I often times do as I travel across campus, and I saw a young woman up ahead. She was heading toward me up a long, slightly-sloped area of campus, and, being a heavy-set woman in a wheelchair, she was having some troubles making the lengthy incline. She was on the same sidewalk as me and was heading my way, but I turned along my usual route, and ended up on a parallel sidewalk some distance from her. I had noticed that she was beginning to struggle continuing up this inclined area, but I had to get to my class. I could not help but watch her as I walked on, waiting to see if anyone was going to help her.

I kept turning around, even as she was nearly two-hundred feet behind me, and kept watching as she struggled more and more. Eventually, she was barely moving and it was all she could do to keep inching forward. The thing that most upset me was the fact that she was getting passed on a busy sidewalk like a bicyclist on the highway. It was like everyone refused to see what was going on. I was so aggravated, but then remembered my own selfishness. I had turned from meeting her head on, even though I could easily tell she had needed help, because I wanted to make it to my class on time.

Frustration overcame me as I witnessed hundreds of people do the exact same thing I had just done. They flat out ignored the fact that she could really use a hand. It overwhelmed me, and I turned around to start walking back to help her. It was at that moment, I saw a girl defy the norm, and offer assistance. The girl bent down and smiled, and was talking to the woman in the wheelchair as she began to push her. "Finally," I said to myself.

Guilt crawled all over my mind as I walked the rest of the way to class. I had avoided having to help her so that I could make it to my class on time; that same class that I was getting to walk to all by myself with no extra assistance needed. I told myself right at that moment that this was not going to happen again, and that things would play out differently if I were given the same sort of opportunity again. It really is surreal how things seem to play out sometimes.

Two days later, in almost the exact same spot, she was coming up the beginning of the sloped sidewalk. This time, I did not even think about glancing at my phone to check what time it may have been. I walked straight toward her, with a slight smile on my face. I was going to take myself out of the equation for a moment. As she pushed herself up the slope, I could tell she was beginning to get tired by the time I got near her. I walked right up to her, and offered to help her to class. She thanked me, but said it was not even necessary, and she proceeded to point out the fact that I was going the other way. She did not want to inconvenience me.

I gladly turned her rebuttal down, told her that my professor did not care if I was late (I honestly do not remember if that was true or not), and that I did not mind in the least bit. I commandeered the wheelchair, and assisted her all the way up the sloped area and into the adjacent building where her class was. This building did not even have an automated door for handicapped individuals. I could not have imagined her having to open this door by herself and wheel herself though the doorway, after making all that effort just to get there. She was so appreciative when I had gotten her inside, and she thanked me several times before we parted ways. I let her know, big smile and all, that she did not owe me a single thing in the world.

We had talked about her being a psychology major on the way up the inclined area, and I asked all about her experience there at OSU. She loved it, but was admittedly suffering a bit of Senioritis lately. She giggled about this, and then she mentioned how this part of her class schedule gave her hell every day. She hated this inclined area, and she thanked me at least five times as we traveled on. Her tone and amount of gratitude gave me a sinking feeling that she did not see help very often. Being the emotional guy that I am, it was all I could do to not cry as I was trying to make a sprinkle of a difference in the world.

As I walked away, I just let it all out, and started crying as I walked back across campus. I did not care who saw me, or how weird they found it to be that I was walking across campus and crying at 10:30 in the morning (even though that might have been humorous to witness). I just felt at peace with what I had done, and with myself. I knew this is what I should have done all along and that this is what I stood for. This needed to happen naturally, and not by any kind of force. On the same note, this needed to happen more often.

> "Service to others is the rent you pay for your room here on earth."
>
> —Muhammad Ali

We all hear the phrase *Christmas Miracle,* right? While writing this book, I was able to witness my first sort of *Christmas Miracle* in person, and was also able to serve a part in the magic as well. A good friend of mine, John, was someone that I had the privilege to get to know over the fall semester of 2011. He had made an entire web of friendships in the building of Iba Hall (where we live on campus) in just a few months and is a big part of the community in the building. He is one of those people who knows everyone, and everyone knows him; people just like being around him. Unfortunately most people did not know anything about his personal or home life, and they did not know what he was facing at the time.

John found out in the last few weeks of the fall semester that the scholarships and loans he thought were sufficient enough to pay for his schooling were not going to cover all of his bills for the semester. He was hurled into a financial crisis and instantly had a lot more bearing down on his shoulders than just his final exams.

On top of this, his dad was in and out of the hospital with heart issues, and at the time of discovering about the finances, his dad was in a coma after an operation that he had. John could not afford this unexpected need for funds, could not do anything with his dad in the hospital, and was mentally preparing not to be able to come back to college after Christmas Break. He was heart-broken, and very frustrated.

A mutual friend of ours, Bo, and I thought of an idea. The amount of money that John needed was a lot for *one* individual college kid to dish out, but not for a lot of them. We were unsure if we could gather up the amount we needed in time for him to be able to enroll for the next semester, but we were optimistic. Something had to be done, and we were not going to let this take him away from college, not like this. We had to do something for John. He would have done the same for us.

Bo instantly started asking other people who lived in our building if they could help us out at all. I was nervous at first, but was later relieved when the replies started coming back positively. This wish started to become a reality when we started realizing that people were giving us more money than we were asking, and that the total amount was actually rising quicker than we had anticipated. In two days we had acquired everything, and we all got incredibly excited. Overnight, this had become such an amazing thing to have taken part in, and something that greatly inspired me.

We kept most of the names confidential, but a few of us sat him down and told him what we wanted to give him. He was in sincere disbelief. He leaned in for a hug as he good-naturedly told us how much he hated us. He instantly called his dad, who had recently awakened from his coma. His dad instantly started crying and was amazed at how people had come together and how much they cared for his son. The people who helped John out truly gave out of the kindness of their hearts and gave forth their own money for a cause and a person that they believed in. A group of fellow students, all by themselves, helped change someone's life. Living for others has a lot of faces, and this one was a magnificently beautiful portrait.

We are a lot like ants. Each little ant, by themselves, can only do so much. We can fulfill countless small acts of selflessness in our daily lives. I have been striving to become more selfless as time goes on, and something I have thought about is this: all it takes is one tiny little ant to start carrying a big load, and then the whole colony is on the scene to lend a hand and lighten the load. We could be buying someone's food or drink just because, going out of our way to hold the door open for strangers, setting aside our To-Do list to listen to a friend in need, volunteering at a local camp for lesser-privileged children, donating clothes or food to others, working a charity event, or even something so simple and little as donating five dollars to a local cause. It does not have to be our entire estate that we put up for grabs; every little bit counts, especially to those in need. In the case of living for others, quantity is just as important as quality.

The power of an ant is something to be marveled at, and modeled. An ant can do a lot of heavy-lifting on its own, but when the entire colony pitches in, things really get moving. The same could be said for us. Are you one of the individuals that believe a five dollar donation is useless and a waste? What if everyone in a large city (or colony) donated five dollars? That is a lot of money from just one city. Five dollars a week, from each three-hundred-and-something-million Americans, would be over a billion dollars each week. This could be donated to all sorts of causes, in every corner of our nation, and all parts of the world. That is just five dollars every seven days from one country. Imagine the results in different sizes and time scales. It is truly amazing, and it just goes to show that when everyone contributes, even a little bit, we can make big things happen. It seems so easy, and like such a reality, that if we come together, we could change the world in less than a week.

Now it is your turn. How will you make a difference, not just for yourself, but for those around you?

AN INFORMAL GOODBYE

There are many things to be said in the ending of a book like this. In an attempt to show how we can translate and apply these 21 Pillars to any situation in our lives, I am going to mirror each of these Pillars on the book itself. The Pillars are put in the same order that they are arranged in the book, not by importance or chronological occurrence.

Opinions Are Not Facts—This whole book is filled with my opinions. These 21 Pillars, their content, and each of my recommendations are all parts of my opinion about what would help all of us, including myself, become better-rounded individuals as we grow older and make our way through life. In fact, my opinion that this is a neat and interesting way to end the book is merely another opinion of mine.

Everything Changes—A lot changed in the ten months it took to write this. I switched from being a junior to a senior in college, had two different girlfriends, made a bunch of new close friends, secured a post-college job with Teach For America, experienced my parents split their thirty-six year marriage, among other things. There are very few things in my life that are the same as they were when I began writing this book, and that is just me. I trust that everyone reading this went through their own fair share of changes over the last ten months, both big and small.

Appreciate Now, Not Later—As I wrote this book and began my senior year of college, I tried to make time to visit and be around those I love and enjoy. When I would get invited to hang out with people, I would always try to say yes. I tried to remember that I would only have a limited time to keep seeing these people on a regular basis. I had to appreciate my time here in college, and write this book in between. Nothing lasts forever.

Maintain Time for Yourself—Between the two internships I worked while writing this, the classes I was attending, my Residential Life position on campus, and trying to balance all of my other time obligations, I had to take time to occasionally unplug and take a break. Sometimes, I just had to say no to my urges to always be productive.

Apathy is Dangerous—There have been several things that called for action while I wrote this book. I have been more adamant to stop hate speech when I hear it now. I do not think it is appropriate so I try to take a stand, even if on a case-by-case basis. I also secured my position with Teach for America to become a part of the force attempting to bridge the education gap here in America. Apathy is a disease that takes away the exercise of being human. Find your cure.

Keep Responsibility—To complete a book like this in the middle of the unlimited distractions that college can present was a sincere situation of accountability. I promised myself that I would get this book done by graduation and holding myself accountable definitely helped me complete this whole thing in ten months. And not to mention, the professor discussed in this chapter helped me with the book's overall concept a little bit.

Stay Humble—I tried to not bring up my book out of context as I worked on it. I did not walk around and say, "Oh hey, I'm a twenty-one year old college student who is writing his first book. Look how cool I am." I also did not write this from a perspective where I was looking down from a mighty throne telling everyone how to change and orient their lives. I sincerely tried to relate that I, as much as anyone else, am still learning from these Pillars every day.

Count Your Blessings—Let me attempt to count all of the blessings that allowed me to compose and work on this book. I have two arms and hands, a fully-functioning mind, free time to write, motivation to keep going, a desktop computer and laptop that allowed me to write in several types of environments, appropriate stories to complete these chapters, the college education and environment that allowed me to contemplate these kinds of things, a country that would allow me to do such a thing, and friends who helped me along the way, especially Nick Erdogan, my best friend and the editor of this book. This is just the beginning of the list.

Criticism Comes From Solidity—Several people commented, behind my back most of the time, that this book was going to be a failure. They doubted I would even finish such an endeavor. The guy I mentioned in *Appreciate Now Not Later* told some of my friends, "No I won't let him use my name in his stupid book, which won't get done anyway." People made fun of me for my concept I chose to write about. But you know, I loved writing this book, and did so with a big, goofy smile on my face.

Hold Respect For Others—As I wrote about some of the people and situations that frustrated me in this book, I tried to stay respectful on and off these pages. I have tried to hold respect for many of the people I have disagreed with in the course of this book, including the guy who threatened to kill me in October of 2011. He was having a rough sophomore year of school and I tried to hold respect for him.

Harbor Love Not Hate—The girl mentioned in this chapter is still a frequent vent of frustration of mine. When thinking back on those memories, or talking about her with friends, I often get mad pretty quickly. I am still working on this and will continue to do so. I need to forgive as easily as I accept forgiveness. I tried to greet stressful and aggravating situations over the past year with a smile, and not a grimace of hatred.

Confront Your Weaknesses—My weaknesses with this book included some of my limited vocabulary, being a novice writer, and sometimes giving up too easily on those evenings saturated with writer's block. And let us not forget the weakness that was included in the chapter, my public speaking. I have dealt with several very scary presentations during the course of writing this book. Some of them I feel I did pretty well on, and others left me with a shaky voice and quivering knees that were painfully obvious as I tried to compose myself in front of the class.

Stay At Face Value—In my pursuit to stay true to this Pillar, I have reexamined my love for Lamborghinis that I have held since childhood. While writing this book I have seen that they are a status symbol, like the ones I mention in the chapter. I would be a hypocrite to buy one (not that I could anytime soon, anyway). I resisted my urges to buy a lot of different things in the past year that I knew I did not need. I also tried to keep true to myself, and dress just for me. I still wear my band shirts, even now in my senior year of college, and they spur conversation pretty frequently. Professors seem to really enjoy discussing the good ole' days of Nirvana.

Learn From Your Mistakes—I made plenty of mistakes as I wrote this book. From the poor writing habits and grammatical errors, to other things like handling a brief relationship poorly and trying to cut corners in school. I tried to take things from each of these mistakes, and I tried to keep adding to my library of life lessons. I hope to never stop learning about myself, as well as the world around me.

Empathy Not Envy—I encountered many conversations about money while writing this book, and it is something that still tugs at me. I have heard people who are having their college completely paid for by their parents gripe about having to go to class or having to wake up early. I have seen people younger than me driving around the campus here at OSU in cars that could rival the tag price of my house. I strive to keep in mind that they, just like me, were born into their situation. What matters is what they do with what they have. I would not know anything about that until I got to know them.

Be Entrepreneurial—No one asked me to write a book. This was an idea and then a decision of mine made on a long snow day in the early spring of 2011, and that is when I proactively began this journey. I identified an opportunity for a book like this because I had never seen one quite like this before. I thought that a self-help style book written by a young adult intending to help out other young adults would be a fresh concept. I combined my writing abilities with my personal memories and stories, and my best friend Nick as an editor, and started filling up the pages.

Challenge Your Perceptions—Writing this book definitely helped me challenge a few of my perceptions. I think I may be starting to see what the friend mentioned in the chapter was saying about how arrogant people are the actual victims. It is too bad they often cover it up with a sulfuric attitude. I have been testing my perceptions on many other things while living out my last years in college preparing for the future.

Chase Your Passion—Writing this book was chasing a passion of mine. I wanted to help people, share with them my story, and I have come to love writing. Filmmaking takes so many resources and is so hard to coordinate, but writing can be done on my own time and with much fewer restraints. My passion for pursuing a career in filmmaking has been shifting over towards aspirations of becoming a writer. I think my next book will be fiction, and maybe someday I will get a book published. The Teach for America position I obtained also allows me to chase my passion by continuing to help people; young children in need of an education, that is.

Hold the Diamonds of Others—I have had some hills and valleys with friends of mine while writing this book, but I always tried to keep the bigger picture in mind. Disputes and disagreements should not erase the past, and a friendship is something worth fighting for, but there is also always a limit. I am still close friends with Steven, the individual mentioned in this chapter. When I graduate soon and move away, we will no longer be able to hang out on a regular basis. I try to cherish the time left with all of my friends like this. We have to hold onto these diamonds of others, and wear them for all to see.

Keep Tenacity—Writing your first book in itself while in college and working different jobs takes tenacity. Trust me; there were plenty of times when I felt like giving up. I wanted to just stop writing altogether. It was hard to keep going, and I often felt like I would never complete it. But fortunately, drive and motivation kept me going and ta da, it is finished. I owe the completion of this book to tenacity and the force that it carries with it.

Live For Others—All I have to say about this Pillar and how it pertains to this book is this: if this book is either enjoyed by or helps at least one person in their life, then every ounce of energy expelled to make this entire thing was so worth it. End of story.

These 21 Pillars were just my set of poles holding up my foundation. So, what are yours? How do you plan to shape tomorrow with what you can do today? There are countless people you will meet, situations you will encounter, problems you will overcome, and things you will learn. It is going to be a crazy journey for us all. One thing I can say for sure is that I hope you can take these Pillars and my stories to mind and heart, and that you can use them for the road ahead. *Your* road ahead.

I would like to ask a favor of you as well. That favor would be for you to be unique in life, and do incredible things for the world and those around you. Whether or not it is because of something you read in this book or not, I just hope you do not end up being the classic middle-aged person who hates their job, regrets their past, and has no excitement for the future.

Do not drift through life as just one more person who lives life based on everyone else. Create. Harvest. Innovate. Inspire. Change the world. Do you think it is dumb to say *change the world*? I have said that this is one of my goals in life, and I have been made fun of for it. There was a quote I found by Steve Jobs during the end of writing this book that says it perfectly: "Those crazy enough to think they can change the world, end up doing so." You know what I say? Let's be crazy. All of us.

Now that you have read the Pillars that this book has to offer, what now? The work is not done. In fact, it is just about to begin and it lasts for the rest of your life. The ending of this book is not supposed to be something you think about for a day and then never act upon. The ending of this book should be the intro to your own book; your life story. "Life is a novel with the ending tore out," stated James Frey. Let us get to writing. Not tomorrow, or next year for a new year's resolution. Today.

Be the teacher who inspires those who listen. Be that favorite music people listen to in order to escape and relax. Be the party that people attend so that they can laugh and have a good weekend. Be the teddy bear someone clings to on tough days. Be the performer that people flock to be able to witness in action. Be the person of hope who speaks quietly into a microphone after a nation's tragedy.

Be the song at the end of a movie that always leaves people with a smile on their face. And be the quote people write on their walls to inspire themselves every day. Defy the odds, swim upstream, and be an agent of change.

> "Be the change you wish to see in the world."
> —Mahatma Gandhi

Thank you for reading.